AF408453

INSTANT POT COOKBOOK FOR TWO

Easy, Delicious and Healthy Instant Pot Recipes for Two

Savannah Gibbs

The trademarks that are used are without any consent, and the publication of the trademark is without permission or backing by the trademark owner. All trademarks and brands within this book are for clarifying purposes only and are owned by the owners themselves, not affiliated with this document.

Table of Contents

CHAPTER SIX

CHAPTER SEVEN

Introduction

If you love cooking from home, you certainly have heard of Instant Pot. For starters, it's a modern pressure cooker that helps you cook tasty foods such as chicken, vegetables, dried beans, seafood, and even yogurt at lightning fast speed. The appliance can save you up to 70% off your cooking time compared to other cooking methods.

When you use an Instant Pot to cook broccoli, steam surrounds the broccoli so that it is not oxidized by air. Therefore, the broccoli will retain its natural green color and preserve its nutrients, making it a healthy food to eat. As an Instant Pot is completely sealed, it will not create a mess in your home and kitchen with smell or steam. This makes Instant Pot an ideal and convenient cooking device for two people.

Whether you are cooking for yourself, a guest, or loved one, this book offers a great collection of new ideas that you'll want to try. You'll learn 100 healthy and delicious recipes for breakfast, poultry, meats, seafood, vegetables, beans, soups, snacks, and dessert. These recipes are easy to follow and are designed for two people. All you need to do is buy the ingredients, dump them in the pot, and allow it to work its magic.

CHAPTER ONE

Introduction of the Instant Pot

A new trend among people who eat healthy and enjoy cooking with minimal mess and time is the modern pressure cooker, Instant Pot. This type of cooking instrument has been around for several decades, but new models have come to the market vastly improved, and with health and convenience in mind.

In addition to pressure cooking, the Instant Pot can also be used as a slow cooker, rice cooker, stove, steamer, and sauté pan. It is this ability to wear many hats that makes the Instant Pot so popular. There's no need to spend hours in the kitchen, standing over multiple pots and pans.

Benefits of Using Instant Pot

Cook faster

If you're not familiar with the mechanics of a pressure cooker, they're pretty simple. The food is cooked inside a pot at high heat, and the steam that builds up inside that sealed environment conducts all the cooking. The heat and the pressure rise from the heating source throughout the pot. Because the Instant Pot is a sealed container, the temperature of the liquids in the pot can exceed that of boiling water. Because the food is in a hotter environment, it cooks faster. Using an Instant Pot can reduce your cooking time by a whopping 70%.

Easy to use

The menu interface on the front of the Instant Pot has settings that are similar to a microwave oven, and very easy to use. In fact, a 6-year-old will have no problem learning how to cook with this device.

Preservation of the nutritional value of food

The longer you cook food, the more you're cooking off valuable ingredients such as vitamins, minerals, and proteins. Instant Pot cooking will not do that to your food. Since the Instant Pot is designed to evenly distribute steam, there is no need to immerse food in water. All you have to do is fill the bottom of the pot with enough water to create steam. This helps tremendously when it comes to preserving nutrients in the food, which water otherwise washes away.

Environment friendly

Another benefit is that the Instant Pot is environmentally sound. You're using less energy with this cooking tool than you would use with your oven or stovetop. The one-pot cooking technology will reduce your cleanup and your electric or gas bill. It also keeps your kitchen cooler.

How to Use an Instant Pot

Familiarize yourself with pressure release methods

There are two ways to release pressure in an Instant Pot: the "quick pressure release" or the "natural pressure release." The "quick pressure release" happens when the pressure valve is opened manually, and the steam is released quickly. As the steam is released, so is the pressure. When all of the pressure is released, the float valve sinks and the lid is unlocked. For safety's sake, there is no way for the lid to open until the float valve drops. Some steam will be given off, so don't stick your face too close just yet.

The "natural pressure release" happens when you let the pressure decrease without opening the pressure valve. After the allotted cooking time, the Instant Pot automatically switches from cooking mode to the "Keep Warm" mode. During this time, the pressure naturally drops. How long this takes depends on how much liquid is in the pot. It can take anywhere from ten minutes to half an hour. The float valve will drop when it is time.

What specific release method should you use? For vegetables, it is best to use the "quick pressure release," since vegetables will get soggy if overcooked. The "natural pressure release" method is a great way to let meats, soups, and stews simmer.

Familiarize yourself with Instant Pot buttons

There are manual settings, as well as a full range of pre-selected cooking routines that you can program with the push of a single button. A timer can even delay the start time for up to 24 hours. Below are the standard buttons that make using the Instant Pot such a pleasure:

Manual: this setting is used when you want to adjust the pressure and cooking time. The majority of recipes in this book use the Manual setting.

Sauté: this sautés and can be adjusted up to **frying** and down to **simmer.** This function is also used to reheat food and to thicken sauces.

Slow Cook: this function turns the Instant Pot into a slow cooker. When using this setting, you must turn the pressure release handle to the Venting position.

Keep Warm/Cancel: this will cancel a prior function, while keeping the food warm.

Soup: this function prepares soups for 40 minutes at high pressure. The time can be manually adjusted by using the "-" or "+" buttons.

Meat/Stew: this setting prepares meats for 35 minutes at high pressure. Cooking time can be adjusted manually.

Bean/Chili: this prepares beans for 30 minutes at high pressure. Cooking time can be adjusted manually.

Poultry: this cooks chicken for 15 minutes at high pressure. Cooking time can be adjusted manually.

Rice: this prepares rice; the cooking time cannot be adjusted manually.

Multigrain: this cooks at high pressure for 40 minutes. Cooking time can be adjusted manually.

Porridge: this cooks oatmeal or porridge at high pressure for 20 minutes. Cooking time can be adjusted manually.

Steam: this is used to steam foods such as vegetables in a steamer basket. It cooks at high pressure for 10 minutes.

Tips for Cooking in Instant Pot

While it does many things with ease, the Instant Pot is especially well-suited towards the creation of soups, chilis, and stews made from scratch. Its ability to soften up unsoaked beans, while all the other ingredients cook, is a real bonus for busy people. It can also turn even the toughest cut of meat into fall-off-the-bone perfection in very short order, which makes it ideal for things such as spare ribs.

Make sure you use enough liquid when you're cooking, and don't try to fry anything in it because oil can damage the system.

Keep it simple at the start

It's going to take you a while to familiarize yourself with the variety of functions with which an Instant Pot is equipped. If you are a first-time user, you need to keep things simple. Rather than trying your hand at a complex cooking method, try something easy first, like boiling eggs or warming up a dish.

Remember added time

It will take about 10 minutes for your Instant Pot to come to pressure. For example, if it takes 20 minutes of cooking at high pressure, then you'll need to add 10 minutes to the total cooking time. You will also need to add 10 to 20 minutes for natural pressure release (depending on how much food you have in the pot). Even a quick pressure release can take a few minutes. You don't need to add cook time if you're using the slow cooker or sauté option.

Because of the time lag involved in both starting and stopping the pressure cooking process, fish and seafood have to be treated with particular care since many of these ingredients can turn either mushy or rubbery if overcooked.

Get extra parts

The Instant Pot comes with a stainless steel inner pot, however, getting an extra inner pot could help you to prepare two different dishes. Also, if you use the Instant Pot quite often, then you will always have one inner pot available for use while the other is being cleaned in the dishwasher.

You can also cook with different lids. You can actually get a glass lid, which is similar to a slow cooker lid. You can use this lid when you're using the sauté or slow cooker functions. The glass lid cannot be used for the pressure cooking function.

Clean it regularly

Just because it takes less time to cook, does not mean that it doesn't require frequent cleaning. Fortunately, this appliance is very easy to clean, as the inner pot is easily detachable. Make it a habit to clean your Instant Pot after each use.

About the Recipes in This Book

In this book, you will find 100 healthy and delicious recipes that each contain nutritional information. If a recipe doesn't need a fixed quantities of salt (for example, "Salt to taste"), the salt/sodium information is not included in that recipe, as each person has a different taste. These Instant Pot recipes are designed for two people, and most of the recipes make two servings. There are a few recipes that make more than 2 servings, so that you can refrigerate or freeze the leftovers for later.

CHAPTER TWO

Breakfast

Creamy Coconut Oats

Yield: 2 servings
Preparation Time: 2 minutes
Cooking Time: 4 minutes
Ingredients:
¼ cup coconut flakes, unsweetened
½ cup steel cut oats
½ cup coconut milk + more for topping
1 cup water
Sea salt to taste
1 tablespoon brown sugar
¼ teaspoon ground cinnamon

Directions:
1. Add the coconut flakes to the Instant Pot and select SAUTÉ. Cook for 2–3 minutes, stirring frequently, until lightly brown. Remove half of the coconut to set aside.

2. Add in oats, toasting until fragrant.

3. Add the coconut milk, reserving some for topping. Stir in the rest of the ingredients. Mix to combined well.

4. Close the lid and cook at high pressure for 2 minutes.

5. When cooking is complete, do a natural pressure release.

6. Serve warm drizzled with coconut milk and toasted coconut.

Nutritional Information (Per Serving)
Calories: 218
Fat: 12.3g

Sat. Fat: 10g
Carbohydrates: 23.5g
Fiber: 4.1g
Sugar: 5.6g
Protein: 4.4g

Blueberry Bowl

Yield: 2 servings
Preparation Time: 1 hour 10 minutes
Cooking Time: 1 minutes
Ingredients:
½ tablespoon honey + extra for serving
¾ cup water
1 small cinnamon stick
¾ cup white quinoa
⅛ cup raisins
½ cup apples, grated
½ cup apple juice
½ cup plain yogurt
⅛ cup pistachios, chopped
3 tablespoons blueberries

Directions:
1. Rinse the quinoa and strain it through a fine mesh strainer.

2. Add the water and cinnamon stick to your Instant Pot, locking the lid. Cook at high pressure for 1 minutes.

3. When cooking is complete, allow pressure to release naturally for 10 minutes. Quick release the remaining pressure.

4. Spoon the quinoa into a bowl and remove the cinnamon stick. Allow it to cool, then add the apple, apple juice, raisins, and honey. Stir to combine.

5. Refrigerate for at least 1 hour or overnight.

6. Add the yogurt, stirring well.

7. Serve topped with honey and blueberries.

Nutritional Information (Per Serving)
Calories: 416
Fat: 6.4g
Sat. Fat: 1.3g
Carbohydrates: 74.3g
Fiber: 6.8g
Sugar: 25.4g
Protein: 13.8g
Sodium: 73mg

Creamy Eggs

Yield: 2 servings
Preparation Time: 10 minutes
Cooking Time: 2 minutes
Ingredients:
2 tablespoons cream

2 eggs
½ tablespoon fresh chives, minced
Salt and pepper to taste

Directions:
1. Grease 2 ramekins.

2. Place 1 tablespoon of cream in each prepared ramekin.

3. Carefully crack 1 egg into each ramekin and sprinkle with chives.

4. Arrange the trivet in the Instant Pot. Add 1 cup of water in Instant Pot.

5. Place the ramekins on top of trivet.

6. Secure the lid and place the pressure valve to the SEAL position.

7. Press the MANUAL button and cook at high pressure for 2 minutes.

8. When cooking is complete, do a quick pressure release.

9. Remove the lid and transfer the ramekins onto serving plates.

10. Sprinkle with salt and black pepper and serve immediately.

Nutritional Information (Per Serving)
Calories: 71
Fat: 5.1g
Sat Fat: 1.8g
Carbohydrates: 0.8g
Fiber: 0g
Sugar: 0.6g
Protein: 5.7g

Eggs in Cups

Yield: 2 servings
Preparation Time: 15 minutes
Cooking Time: 4 minutes
Ingredients:
2 bell peppers
2 eggs
Salt and pepper to taste
1 tablespoon mozzarella cheese, grated freshly
2 bread slices, toasted

Directions:
1. With a sharp knife, cut the bell peppers ends to form about 1½-inch high cup, and remove the seeds.
2. Crack 1 egg in each bell pepper cup. Cover each bell peppers with a piece of foil.
3. Arrange a steamer basket in the Instant Pot. Add 1½ cups of water in the Instant Pot.
4. Arrange bell pepper cups in steamer basket.
5. Close the lid and cook at low pressure for 4 minutes.
6. After cooking is complete, carefully do a quick pressure release.
7. Remove the lid and transfer the bell pepper cups onto serving plates.
8. Sprinkle with salt, pepper, and cheese.
9. Serve immediately alongside bread slices.

Nutritional Information (Per Serving)
Calories: 165
Fat: 7.5g
Sat Fat: 2.9g
Carbohydrates: 14.4g
Fiber: 1.8g
Sugar: 6.7g
Protein: 11.4g

Omelet Cups

Yield: 2 servings
Preparation Time: 15 minutes
Cooking Time: 8 minutes
Ingredients:

2 eggs
1 tablespoon fresh cilantro, minced
½ of small jalapeño pepper, seeded and minced
Salt and pepper to taste
½ cup cooked chicken, chopped finely
½ scallion, chopped
2 tablespoons cheddar cheese, shredded

Directions:
1. Lightly grease 2 silicon muffin cups. Keep aside.
2. In a bowl, add eggs, jalapeño pepper, cilantro, salt, and pepper and beat until well combined.
3. In another bowl, mix together chicken, scallion, and cheese.
4. Divide the chicken mixture into prepared muffin cups. Pour egg mixture over chicken mixture evenly and stir to combine.
5. Arrange a steamer trivet in the Instant Pot. Add 1½ cups of water in the Instant Pot.
6. Place the muffin cups on top of the trivet.
7. Secure the lid and cook at low pressure for 8 minutes.
8. After cooking is complete, use a quick pressure release.
9. Remove the lid and transfer the muffin cups onto serving plates.
10. Serve warm.

Nutritional Information (Per Serving)
Calories: 147
Fat: 7.8g

Sat Fat: 3.2g
Carbohydrates: 1g
Fiber: 0.2g
Sugar: 0.6g
Protein: 17.6g

Mushroom Frittata

Yield: 2 servings
Preparation Time: 15 minutes
Cooking Time: 3 minutes
Ingredients:
¾ cup sharp cheddar cheese, shredded and divided
3 eggs
¾ cup fresh mushrooms, chopped
3 tablespoons half-and-half
Salt and pepper to taste
1 tablespoon fresh cilantro, chopped

Directions:
1. In a bowl, add half of the cheese and remaining ingredients, and mix well.
2. Divide mixture into 2 (½-pint) wide mouth jars and sprinkle with remaining cheese.
3. Cover the jars with lids loosely.
4. Arrange a steamer trivet in the Instant Pot. Add 2 cups of water in the Instant Pot.
5. Place the jars on top of trivet.
6. Secure the lid and cook at high pressure for 3 minutes.
7. After the cooking is complete, carefully do a quick pressure release.
8. Remove the lid and serve immediately.

Nutritional Information (Per Serving)
Calories: 300
Fat: 23.3g
Sat Fat: 12.6g
Carbohydrates: 2.9g
Fiber: 0.3g
Sugar: 1.2g
Protein: 20.4g

Sweet Potato Hash

Yield: 2 servings
Preparation Time: 15 minutes
Cooking Time: 16 minutes
Ingredients:
1 cup sweet potato, peeled and cubed
2 tablespoons olive oil
1 small onion, chopped
2 cooked bacon slices, chopped
1 jalapeño pepper, chopped
2 tablespoons fresh cilantro, chopped
Salt and pepper to taste
2 eggs

Directions:
1. Lightly grease a casserole dish. Set aside.

2. In the prepared casserole dish, place the sweet potato.

3. Arrange a steamer trivet in the Instant Pot. Add 1½ cups of water in the Instant Pot.

4. Place the casserole dish on top of trivet.

5. Secure the lid and cook at high pressure for 8 minutes.

6. After cooking is complete, carefully do a quick pressure release.

7. Remove the lid and transfer the cooked sweet potato to a bowl.

8. Remove the trivet from the Power Pressure Cooker and drain the water. With paper towels, pat dry pot.

9. Place the oil in the Instant Pot and select SAUTÉ. Add the onion and cook for 4–5 minutes on high heat.

10. Stir in the cooked sweet potato and remaining ingredients, except eggs.

11. With a spoon, make two wells in the sweet potato mixture. Crack an egg in each well.

12. Press CANCEL, close the lid, and let the mixture cool for 10 minutes.

13. Serve warm.

Nutritional Information (Per Serving)
Calories: 444
Fat: 30.6g
Sat Fat: 7.3g
Carbohydrates: 25.2g
Fiber: 4.3g
Sugar: 8.6g
Protein: 18.6g

Squash & Apple Porridge

Yield: 2 servings
Preparation Time: 20 minutes
Cooking Time: 8 minutes
Ingredients:
1 (1¼-pound) whole delicata squash
2 medium apples, cored and chopped roughly
½ cup chicken broth
½ teaspoon ground cinnamon
⅛ teaspoon ground ginger
⅛ teaspoon ground cloves
2 tablespoons maple syrup
2 tablespoons gelatin
Pinch of salt

Directions:
1. In the Instant Pot, place squash, apples, broth, and spices.

2. Secure the lid and cook at high pressure for 8 minutes.

3. Allow the pressure to release naturally for 10 minutes. Then do a quick pressure release.

4. Remove the lid, let the squash mixture cool, then transfer the squash onto a cutting board.

5. Cut the squash in half lengthwise and remove the seeds.

6. In a blender, add squash, apple mixture from the pot, maple syrup, gelatin and salt, and pulse until smooth.

7. Serve immediately.

Nutritional Information (Per Serving)
Calories: 314
Fat: 0.8g
Sat Fat: 0.1g
Carbohydrates: 45.1g
Fiber: 9.1g
Sugar: 45.3g

Protein: 13.8g
Sodium: 292mg

Nuts Porridge

Yield: 2 servings
Preparation Time: 15 minutes
Cooking Time: 3 minutes
Ingredients:
½ cup unsweetened dried coconut shreds
½ cup raw unsalted cashews
¼ cup pecan halves
¼ cup pepitas, shelled
1 cup water
1 tablespoon maple syrup
2 teaspoons coconut oil, melted

Directions:
1. In a food processor, add coconut shreds, cashews, pecans and pepitas, and pulse until an almond meal like mixture is formed.

2.Transfer the mixture into the Instant Pot and stir in water, maple syrup and oil.

3. Secure the lid and place the pressure valve to the SEAL position.

4. Press the PORRIDGE button.

5. After the cooking is complete, carefully do a quick pressure release.

6. Remove the lid and transfer into serving bowls.

7. Serve warm.

Nutritional Information (Per Serving)
Calories: 530

Fat: 45.7g
Sat Fat: 15.6g
Carbohydrates: 26.2g
Fiber: 5.1g
Sugar: 9.6g
Protein: 11.8g
Sodium: 17mg

Millet Porridge

Yield: 2 servings
Preparation Time: 10 minutes
Cooking Time: 9 minutes
Ingredients:
1 cup water
½ cup millet
1½ tablespoons honey
3 tablespoons fresh blueberries

Directions:
1. In the Instant Pot, mix together water and millet.
2. Secure the lid and cook at high pressure for 10 minutes.
3. After the cooking is complete, use a quick pressure release.
4. Remove the lid and with a fork, fluff the porridge.
5. Drizzle with honey and serve with a topping of blueberries.

Nutritional Information (Per Serving)
Calories: 245
Fat: 2.2g
Sat Fat: 0.4g
Carbohydrates: 51.4g
Fiber: 4.6g
Sugar: 14.3g
Protein: 5.7g
Sodium: 7mg

Pecan Pie Oatmeal

Yield: 2 servings
Preparation Time: 5 minutes
Cooking Time: 3 minutes
Ingredients:
½ cup steel cut oats
1¾ cups water
⅛ cup half & half
2 medjool dates, chopped
¼ cup pecans, chopped
3 tablespoons maple syrup
½ teaspoon ground cinnamon
¼ teaspoon nutmeg

Directions:
1. Add all of the ingredients to your Instant Pot and stir.
2. Close the lid and cook at high pressure for 3 minutes.
3. When the cooking is complete, do a natural pressure release.
4. Serve warm with maple syrup.

Nutritional Information (Per Serving)
Calories: 230
Fat: 8.2g
Sat. Fat: 1.9g
Carbohydrates: 37.1g
Fiber: 3.3g
Sugar: 19.1g
Protein: 4g
Sodium: 16mg

Oats with Caramelized Apples

Yield: 2 servings
Preparation Time: 15 minutes
Cooking Time: 8 minutes
Ingredients:
For Oats:
½ cup old fashioned rolled oats
1 teaspoon butter
1 teaspoon sugar
Pinch of salt
¾ cup milk
¾ cup water

For Caramelized Apples:
½ teaspoon butter
1 large apple, peeled, cored, and sliced
¼ tablespoon. honey
Pinch of brown sugar
Pinch of ground cinnamon

Directions:

1. For oats: in the bottom of an Instant Pot, place all ingredients and stir to combine well.

2. Secure the lid and cook at high pressure for 3 minutes.

4. After the cooking is complete, carefully do a quick pressure release.

5. Meanwhile, for apples: in a nonstick skillet, melt butter over medium heat and cook apple slices for about 4–5 minutes, stirring continuously.

6. Stir in honey and cook for about 2–3 minutes, stirring continuously.

7. Add brown sugar, cinnamon and a splash of water and stir to combine.

8. Increase the heat to medium-high and cook for about 2 minutes more.

9. Remove the lid of the Instant Pot and stir the oats.

10. Serve with the topping of caramelized apples.

Nutritional Information (Per Serving)
Calories: 241
Fat: 6.7g
Sat Fat: 3.2g
Carbohydrates: 40.4g
Fiber: 5.3g
Sugar: 20.6g
Protein: 6.8g
Sodium: 145mg

Quinoa with Strawberries

Yield: 2 servings
Preparation Time: 10 minutes
Cooking Time: 1 minutes
Ingredients:
1 cup plus 2 tablespoons water
¾ cup uncooked quinoa, rinsed
1 cup fresh strawberries, hulled and sliced
¼ cup vanilla Greek yogurt
1 tablespoon honey
¼ teaspoon vanilla extract
⅛ teaspoon pumpkin pie spice

Directions:
1. In the bottom of an Instant Pot, place all ingredients and stir to combine well.
2. Secure the lid and cook at high pressure for 1 minute.
3. When the cooking is complete, allow pressure to release naturally.
4. Remove the lid and with a fork, fluff the quinoa.
5. Serve warm.

Nutritional Information (Per Serving)
Calories: 320
Fat: 4.6g
Sat Fat: 0.7g
Carbohydrates: 58.9g
Fiber: 5.9g
Sugar: 15.1g
Protein: 11.9g
Sodium: 13mg

Breakfast Casserole

Yield: 4 servings
Preparation Time: 5 minutes
Cooking Time: 5 minutes
Ingredients:
6 eggs
1 tablespoon butter
1 tablespoon milk
½ cup water
1 cup chopped ham
6 small red potatoes, chopped

Directions:
1. In a bowl, beat the eggs and milk until fluffy. Add the remaining ingredients to the bowl and stir.

2. Grease a heatproof dish with butter, place the egg mixture in the dish. Cover with foil.

3. Pour 1 cup water into the bottom of the Instant pot. Lower a steam rack and place the dish on the rack.

4. Close the lid, choose MANUAL, and cook at high pressure for 20 minutes.

5. When the cooking is complete, do a natural pressure release.

Nutritional Information (Per Serving)
Calories: 355
Fat: 12.8g
Sat Fat: 5.0g
Carbohydrates: 42.5g
Fiber: 4.8g
Sugar: 3.2g
Protein: 18.9g
Sodium: 571mg

Egg Croissants

Yield: 4 servings
Preparation Time: 5 minutes
Cooking Time: 8 minutes
Ingredients:
4 large eggs
Salt and pepper to taste
4 slices of cooked bacon, broken into small pieces
5 tablespoons shredded cheddar cheese
1 green scallion, diced
4 croissants

Directions:
1. Place a steamer basket inside the Instant Pot and pour in 1½ cups water.

2. Whip the eggs in a bowl. Add the bacon pieces, cheese, and scallion to the eggs. Mix well.

3. Divide the mixture into 4 muffin cups. Transfer the filled muffin cups onto the steamer basket.

4. Shut the lid and cook at high pressure for 8 minutes.

5. When the cooking is complete, do a natural pressure release for 5 minutes. Quick release the remaining pressure.

6. Lift the muffin cups out of the Instant Pot.

7. Slice 4 croissants in half and stuff with the muffin cup content.

Nutritional Information (Per Serving)
Calories: 482
Fat: 29.9g
Sat Fat: 13.8g
Carbohydrates: 31.5g
Fiber: 1.7g
Sugar: 8.0g
Protein: 21.0g

CHAPTER THREE

Soups and Stews

Carrot Soup

Yield: 2 servings
Preparation Time: 15 minutes
Cooking Time: 22 minutes
Ingredients:
1 tablespoon unsalted butter
1 small onion, chopped
½ teaspoon fresh ginger, minced
1 garlic clove, minced
½ pound carrots, peeled and chopped
Salt and pepper to taste
7-ounce canned unsweetened coconut milk
1 cup chicken broth
½ tablespoon Sriracha
⅛ teaspoon brown sugar
1 tablespoon fresh cilantro, chopped

Directions:
1. Place the butter in the Instant Pot and select SAUTÉ. Add the onion and cook for 3 minutes.

2. Add ginger and garlic and cook for 1 minute.

3. Add carrots, salt and black pepper and cook for another 2 minutes.

4. Press CANCEL and stir in coconut milk, broth and Sriracha.

5. Secure the lid and cook at high pressure for 6 minutes.

6. When the cooking is complete, do a natural pressure release for 10 minutes. Quick release the remaining pressure.

7. Remove the lid and stir in the brown sugar.

8. With an immerse blender, puree the soup.

9. Serve immediately with the garnishing of cilantro.

Nutritional Information (Per Serving)
Calories: 367
Fat: 30.2g
Sat Fat: 24.8g
Carbohydrates: 22.2g
Fiber: 5.8g
Sugar: 10.9g
Protein: 6.2g

Minestrone Soup

Yield: 2 servings
Preparation Time: 10 minutes
Cooking Time: 8 minutes
Ingredients:
1 tablespoon olive oil
1 bay leaf
1 onion, diced
¼ cup fresh spinach
Salt and pepper to taste
2 cups chicken broth
½ cup elbow pasta
14 ounces tomatoes, diced
1 cup cooked white beans
1 carrot, diced
1 teaspoon dried basil
1 teaspoon dried oregano
2 garlic cloves, minced

Directions:

1. Program the Instant Pot to SAUTÉ. Pour olive oil into the pot and add carrot, onion, garlic, and celery. Mix and cook until the onion softens.

2. Add oregano, basil, pepper, and salt. Mix to combine.

3. Add tomatoes, spinach, bone broth, pasta, and bay leaf. Press CANCEL.

4. Close the lid and cook at high pressure for 6 minutes.

5. When the cooking is complete, wait for 5 minutes before you do a quick pressure release.

6. Open the lid and add white beans.

7. Serve the soup in bowls.

Nutritional Information (Per Serving)
Calories: 397
Fat: 10.2g
Sat Fat: 1.7g
Carbohydrates: 58.3g
Fiber: 10.3g
Sugar: 10.2g
Protein: 20.7g

Black Beans Curry

Yield: 2 servings
Preparation Time: 15 minutes
Cooking Time: 35 minutes
Ingredients:
1 tablespoon olive oil
1 teaspoon cumin seeds
1 medium onion, chopped
1 tablespoon garlic paste
1 tablespoon ginger paste
2 teaspoons ground coriander
1 teaspoon red chili powder

½ teaspoon ground turmeric
½ teaspoon garam masala
Salt to taste
1 cup black beans, soaked overnight and drained
2 cups water
1 teaspoon fresh lemon juice

Directions:

1. Place the oil in the Instant Pot and select SAUTÉ. Add the cumin seeds and cook for 30 seconds.

2. Add onion, ginger, garlic, and spices and cook for about 3–4 minutes.

3. Press CANCEL and stir in the chickpeas and water.

4. Secure the lid, press the BEAN/CHILI button, and use the default time of 30 minutes.

5. After the cooking is complete, use a natural pressure release.

6. Remove the lid and stir in lemon juice.

7. Serve hot.

Nutritional Information (Per Serving)
Calories: 439
Fat: 9.1g
Sat Fat: 1.5g
Carbohydrates: 70.5g
Fiber: 17g
Sugar: 4.7g
Protein: 22.5g

Pork Soup

Yield: 2 servings
Preparation Time: 20 minutes
Cooking Time: 30 minutes
Ingredients:
1 tablespoon olive oil
½ pound ground pork
1 small onion, chopped
1 cup carrot, peeled and shredded
1½ cups cabbage, chopped
2 cups low-sodium chicken broth
1 tablespoon soy sauce
½ teaspoon ground ginger
Freshly ground black pepper to taste

Directions:
1. Place the oil in the Instant Pot and select SAUTÉ. Add the pork and cook for 5 minutes or until browned.

2. Press CANCEL and stir in the remaining ingredients.

3. Secure the lid and cook at high pressure for 25 minutes.

4. When the cooking is complete, use a quick pressure release.

5. Serve hot.

Nutritional Information (Per Serving)
Calories: 296
Fat: 11.1g
Sat Fat: 2.4g
Carbohydrates: 14.3g
Fiber: 3.6g
Sugar: 6.2g
Protein: 34.2g
Sodium: 637mg

Beef & Potato Stew

Yield: 2 servings
Preparation Time: 15 minutes
Cooking Time: 45 minutes
Ingredients:
1 tablespoon olive oil
½ pound beef stew meat, cut into cubes
1 small onion, chopped
2 carrots, peeled and chopped
2 medium potatoes, chopped
1 celery stalk, chopped
1 cups fresh kale leaves, trimmed and chopped
1½ cups beef broth
1 tablespoon hot sauce
½ teaspoon garlic powder
Salt and pepper to taste

Directions:
1. Place the oil in the Instant Pot and select SAUTÉ. Add the beef and cook for about 4–5 minutes or until browned.

2. Press CANCEL and stir in remaining ingredients.

3. Secure the lid, press the MEAT/STEW button, and use the default time of 40 minutes.

4. When the cooking is complete, do a quick pressure release.

5. Serve hot.

Nutritional Information (Per Serving)
Calories: 506
Fat: 15.4g
Sat Fat: 4g
Carbohydrates: 47.8g
Fiber: 8.1g
Sugar: 7.8g
Protein: 43.7g

Sodium: 993mg

Chicken Chili

Yield: 2 servings
Preparation Time: 20 minutes
Cooking Time: 15 minutes
Ingredients:
1 tablespoon olive oil
1 (6-ounce) skinless, boneless chicken breasts, cubed
1 small onion, chopped
½ sweet potato, peeled and cubed
2 garlic cloves, minced
1 jalapeño pepper, chopped
½ teaspoon dried oregano
1 tablespoon red chili powder
½ teaspoon ground cumin
Salt and pepper to taste
8-ounce canned black beans, drained and rinsed
8-ounce canned diced tomatoes, drained
¼ cup uncooked quinoa
1¾ cups chicken broth
1 tablespoon fresh lemon juice

Directions:
1. Place the oil in the Instant Pot and select SAUTÉ. Add the chicken and cook for 4-5 minutes.

2. With a slotted spoon, transfer the chicken into a bowl.

3. In the pot, add the onion and sweet potato and cook for about 5 minutes.

4. Add the garlic, jalapeño pepper, oregano and spices and cook for 1 minute.

5. Press CANCEL and stir in the cooked chicken and remaining ingredients, except for the lemon juice.

6. Secure the lid and cook at high pressure for 4 minutes.

7. When the cooking is complete, do a natural pressure release for 10 minutes. Quick release the remaining pressure.

8. Serve hot with a drizzling of lemon juice.

Nutritional Information (Per Serving)
Calories: 748
Fat: 15.4g
Sat Fat: 3.3g
Carbohydrates: 102.8g
Fiber: 23.6g
Sugar: 10.1g
Protein: 53.6g
Sodium: 841mg

Chicken and Lentil Soup

Yield: 2 servings
Preparation Time: 10 minutes
Cooking Time: 30 minutes
Ingredients:
3 ounces skinless and boneless chicken thighs
¼ pound lentils, rinsed
3 cups water
1 scallion, chopped
1 small onion, chopped
1 medium tomato, diced
1 clove garlic, minced
⅛ cup cilantro, chopped
¼ teaspoon cumin
Pinch of salt
¼ teaspoon paprika

Directions:
1. Put all the ingredients into the Instant Pot, stir well.
2. Cover the lid, press the SOUP button, and cook for 30 minutes.
3. When the cooking is complete, use the natural pressure release.
4. Shred the chicken and serve warm.

Nutritional Information (Per Serving)
Calories: 427
Fat: 7.6g
Sat Fat: 1.6g
Carbohydrates: 41.1g
Fiber: 19.2g
Sugar: 4.5g
Protein: 48.9g
Sodium: 248mg

Chicken Tortilla Soup

Yield: 2 servings
Preparation Time: 10 minutes
Cooking Time: 20 minutes
Ingredients:
1 medium corn tortilla, chopped into squares
1 cup cooked beans
1 garlic clove, minced
1 medium onion, chopped
½ tablespoon olive oil
⅛ teaspoon cayenne pepper
½ teaspoon ground cumin
1 medium tomato, diced
1 tablespoon fresh cilantro, chopped
1 cup chicken broth
1 cup water
4 ounces boneless chicken breasts
1 cup frozen corn

Directions:
1. Place the oil in the Instant Pot and select SAUTÉ. Add onion and cook until it becomes translucent.

2. Add the tortilla squares, cilantro, and garlic, stir well, and cook for another 1 minute.

3. Add chicken, broth, water, spices, beans, and diced tomatoes. Press CANCEL.

4. Close the lid and cook at high pressure for 8 minutes.

5. When the cooking is complete, do a quick pressure release.

6. Remove the chicken from the pot and shred it with the help of forks and then return it the pot and stir well.

7. Garnish with cilantro and serve.

Nutritional Information (Per Serving)

Calories: 416
Fat: 7.8g
Sat Fat: 2.5g
Carbohydrates: 32.6g
Fiber: 6.8g
Sugar: 7.7g
Protein: 60g
Sodium: 558mg

Black Bean Soup

Yield: 2 servings
Preparation Time: 10 minutes
Cooking Time: 30 minutes
Ingredients:
1 medium onion, diced
1 green bell pepper, diced
1 red bell pepper, diced
¼ pound black beans, rinsed
¼ tablespoon black pepper
¼ tablespoon hot sauce
1 stalk celery
½ tablespoon chili powder
½ tablespoon cumin
1 bay leaf
2 cups chicken broth
¼ tablespoon paprika

Directions:
1. Add all the ingredients in the Instant Pot. Mix to combine.

2. Close the lid and cook at high pressure for 30 minutes.

3. When the cooking is complete, do a natural pressure release.

4. Remove the bay leaf and serve with preferred toppings.

Nutritional Information (Per Serving)
Calories: 309
Fat: 3.4g
Sat Fat: 0.7g
Carbohydrates: 53.4g
Fiber: 12.9g
Sugar: 10.6g
Protein: 19.7g
Sodium: 848mg

Creamy Tomato Soup

Yield: 4 servings
Preparation Time: 5 minutes
Cooking Time: 10 minutes
Ingredients:
6 large tomatoes
1 cup water
1 cup heavy cream
½ cup fresh basil leaves, chopped
1 tablespoon dried oregano
½ teaspoon salt
1 teaspoon white pepper

Directions:
1. Cut the tomatoes into halves and place them in the Instant Pot. Add 1 cup of water.

2. Close the lid and cook at high pressure for 5 minutes.

3. When the cooking is complete, do a natural pressure release.

4. Lift the lid and use an immersion blender to achieve a smooth consistency.

5. Add the cream, herbs and salt and pepper to taste. Mix and serve.

Nutritional Information (Per Serving)
Calories: 158
Fat: 11.8g
Sat Fat: 7.0g
Carbohydrates: 12.6g
Fiber: 4.0g
Sugar: 7.3g
Protein: 3.3g
Sodium: 318mg

Split Pea Soup

Yield: 4 servings
Preparation Time: 10 minutes
Cooking Time: 15 minutes
Ingredients:
1 cup dried split peas
1 cup chicken stock
1 cup water
4 slices Canadian bacon, chopped
1 onion, sliced
2 small red potatoes, chopped
2 cloves garlic, minced
½ cup cream
2 tablespoons fresh parsley
Salt and pepper to taste

Directions:
1. Set the Instant Pot to SAUTÉ. Heat the bacon in the pot and as fat comes off the bacon, stir in the onion and garlic.

2. Add the chicken stock, water, and potatoes.

3. Stir in the cream and the peas until everything is combined.

4. Close the lid and cook at high pressure for 15 minutes.

5. When the cooking is complete, do a natural pressure release.

6. Season with salt and pepper and parsley.

Nutritional Information (Per Serving)
Calories: 366
Fat: 10.5g
Sat Fat: 3.8g
Carbohydrates: 47.8g
Fiber: 14.7g
Sugar: 6.8g
Protein: 21.6g

Sodium: 654mg

CHAPTER FOUR

Vegetables and Beans

Beet Salad

Yield: 2 servings
Preparation Time: 15 minutes
Cooking Time: 25 minutes
Ingredients:
For Salad:
4 medium beets, trimmed
2 cups fresh baby spinach
1 tablespoon balsamic vinegar
1 tablespoon feta cheese, crumbled

For Dressing:
2 tablespoons capers
1 small garlic clove, minced
1 tablespoon fresh parsley, minced
1 tablespoon extra-virgin olive oil
Salt and pepper to taste

Directions:
1. Arrange the trivet in the Instant Pot. Add 1 cup of water in the Instant Pot.

2. Place the beets on top of trivet in a single layer.

3. Secure the lid and cook at high pressure for 20 minutes.

4. When the cooking is complete, do a quick pressure release.

5. Remove the inner pot and rinse the beet under running cold water.

6. Cut the beets in desired size slices and transfer into a salad bowl.

7. Add spinach and drizzle with vinegar.

8. In a bowl, add all dressing ingredients and beat until well combined.

9. Pour dressing over beets mixture and gently toss to coat well.

10. Serve with the topping of cheese.

Nutritional Information (Per Serving)
Calories: 174
Fat: 8.6g
Sat Fat: 18g
Carbohydrates: 22.3g
Fiber: 5g
Sugar: 16.4g
Protein: 5.3g

Brussels Sprout Salad

Yield: 2 servings
Preparation Time: 15 minutes
Cooking Time: 3 minutes
Ingredients:
½ pound Brussels sprouts, trimmed and halved
½ tablespoon unsalted butter, melted
½ cup pomegranate seeds
¼ cup almonds, chopped

Directions:

1. Arrange the steamer basket in the bottom of the Instant Pot. Add 1 cup of the water in the Instant Pot.

2. Arrange the Brussels sprout in steamer basket.

3. Secure the lid and cook at high pressure for 4 minutes.

4. When the cooking is complete, carefully do a quick pressure release.

5. Remove the lid and transfer the Brussels sprouts onto serving plates and drizzle with the melted butter.

6. Top with pomegranate seeds and almonds and serve.

Nutritional Information (Per Serving)
Calories: 174
Fat: 9.2g
Sat Fat: 2.4g
Carbohydrates: 20.1g
Fiber: 6g
Sugar: 6.6g
Protein: 6.7g
Sodium: 49mg

Garlic Mashed Potatoes

Yield: 2 servings
Preparation Time: 5 minutes
Cooking Time: 5 minutes
Ingredients:
2 medium russet potatoes
½ cup vegetable broth
3 garlic cloves, minced
2 tablespoons parsley, chopped
Salt to taste
¼ cup low-fat milk

Directions:
1. Cut the potatoes in medium-sized chunks.
2. Put the chunks into the Instant Pot along with the garlic and broth.
3. Close the lid and cook at high pressure for 5 minutes.
4. When the cooking is complete, do a natural pressure release.
5. Open the lid carefully and with a handheld masher, mash the potato.
6. Add milk, parsley and salt and stir well to combine.
7. Serve hot.

Nutritional Information (Per Serving)
Calories: 177
Fat: 0.9g
Sat Fat: 0.4g
Carbohydrates: 36.9g
Fiber: 5.3g
Sugar: 4.3g
Protein: 6.2g

Spiced Okra

Yield: 2 servings
Preparation Time: 15 minutes
Cooking Time: 7 minutes
Ingredients:
1 tablespoon olive oil
3 garlic cloves, chopped
½ teaspoon cumin seeds
1 medium onion, sliced
1 medium tomato, chopped
1 pound okra, cut into 1-inch pieces
½ cup water
½ teaspoon ground coriander
¼ teaspoon red chili powder
¼ teaspoon ground turmeric
Salt and pepper to taste

Directions:
1. Place the oil in the Instant Pot and select SAUTÉ. Add the garlic and cumin seeds and cook for 1 minute.

2. Add the onion and cook for 4 minutes.

3. Add the remaining ingredients and cook for 1 more minute.

4. Press CANCEL and stir well.

5. Secure the lid and cook at high pressure for 2 minutes.

6. When the cooking is complete, do a quick pressure release.

7. Serve hot.

Nutritional Information (Per Serving)
Calories: 195
Fat: 7.8g
Sat Fat: 1.1g
Carbohydrates: 26.5g

Fiber: 9.5g
Sugar: 7.4g
Protein: 6g

Cabbage with Carrot

Yield: 2 servings
Preparation Time: 20 minutes
Cooking Time: 10 minutes
Ingredients:
1 tablespoon coconut oil
1 small onion, sliced
Salt to taste
1 garlic clove, chopped
½ jalapeño pepper, seeded and chopped
½ tablespoon mild curry powder
½ medium head cabbage, shredded
1 small carrot, peeled and sliced
¼ cup desiccated unsweetened coconut
1 tablespoon fresh lemon juice
⅓ cup water

Directions:
1. Place the coconut oil in the Instant Pot and select SAUTÉ. Add the onion and salt and cook for 4 minutes.

2. Add the garlic, jalapeño and curry powder and cook for 1 minute.

3. Press CANCEL and stir in remaining ingredients.

4. Secure the lid and cook at high pressure for 5 minutes.

5. When the cooking is complete, do a natural pressure release for 5 minutes. Quick release the remaining pressure.

6. Serve warm.

Nutritional Information (Per Serving)
Calories: 185
Fat: 10.7g
Sat Fat: 9g
Carbohydrates: 22.2g
Fiber: 8.6g
Sugar: 10.9g
Protein: 4.3g

Green Beans with Mushrooms

Yield: 2 servings
Preparation Time: 20 minutes
Cooking Time: 16 minutes
Ingredients:
½ pound fresh green beans, trimmed
½ tablespoons butter
4-ounce bacon, chopped
½ of small onion, chopped
1 garlic clove, minced
4-ounce fresh mushrooms, sliced
1 teaspoon red wine vinegar
Salt and pepper to taste

Directions:
1. In the Instant Pot, add green beans and enough water to cover.

2. Secure the lid and cook at high pressure for 2 minutes.

3. When cooking is complete, use a quick pressure release.

4. Remove the lid and drain the green beans into a colander.

5. Remove all water from the pot and with paper towels, pat dry it.

11. Place the butter in the Instant Pot and select SAUTÉ. Add the bacon and cook for 3–4 minutes.

12. Add onion and garlic and cook for 2 minutes.

13. Add mushrooms and cook for 5–6 more minutes.

14. Stir in green beans, vinegar, salt, and black pepper and cook for 1 minutes.

15. Press CANCEL and serve hot.

Nutritional Information (Per Serving)
Calories: 389
Fat: 26.9g

Sat Fat: 9.6g
Carbohydrates: 12.9g
Fiber: 4.9g
Sugar: 3.3g
Protein: 25.2g

Spinach with Tomatoes

Yield: 2 servings
Preparation Time: 15 minutes
Cooking Time: 4 minutes
Ingredients:
1 tablespoon olive oil
1 small onion, chopped
1 teaspoon garlic, minced
5 cups fresh spinach, chopped
½ cup tomatoes, chopped
¼ cup tomato puree
¾ cup vegetable broth
½ tablespoon fresh lemon juice
¼ teaspoon red pepper flakes, crushed
Salt and pepper to taste

Directions:
1. Place the oil in the Instant Pot and select SAUTÉ. Add the onion and cook for about 3 minutes.

2. Add the garlic and red pepper flakes and cook for 1 minute.

3. Add spinach and cook for 2 minutes.

4. Press the CANCEL button and stir in the remaining ingredients.

5. Secure the lid and cook at high pressure for 6 minutes.

6. When the cooking is complete, carefully do a quick pressure release.

7. Serve warm.

Nutritional Information (Per Serving)
Calories: 129
Fat: 8.1g
Sat Fat: 1.3g
Carbohydrates: 11.6g
Fiber: 3.7g
Sugar: 4.9g
Protein: 5.4g

Garlicky Bell Peppers

Yield: 2 servings
Preparation Time: 20 minutes
Cooking Time: 5 minutes
Ingredients:
1 tablespoon olive oil
4 garlic cloves, minced
1 jalapeño pepper, seeded and chopped
1 green bell pepper, seeded and cut into long strips
1 red bell pepper, seeded and cut into long strips
1 yellow bell pepper, seeded and cut into long strips
1 orange bell pepper, seeded and cut into long strips
Salt and pepper to taste
½ cup water
1 tablespoon fresh lemon juice

Directions:
1. Place the oil in the Instant Pot and select SAUTÉ. Add the garlic and jalapeño and cook for 1 minute.

2. Press CANCEL and stir in remaining ingredients, except lemon juice.

3. Secure the lid and cook at high pressure for 2 minutes.

4. When the cooking is complete, use a quick pressure release.

5. Remove the lid and select SAUTÉ.

6. Stir in lemon juice and cook for 1–2 minutes.

7. Press CANCEL and serve.

Nutritional Information (Per Serving)
Calories: 149
Fat: 7.7g
Sat Fat: 1.1g
Carbohydrates: 20.6g
Fiber: 3.6g
Sugar: 12.5g

Protein: 2.9g

Curried Edamame

Yield: 2 servings
Preparation Time: 15 minutes
Cooking Time: 18 minutes
Ingredients:
2 teaspoons coconut oil
1 teaspoon black mustard seeds
¼ teaspoon fennel seeds
¼ teaspoon fenugreek seeds
10 curry leaves, chopped roughly
½ cup red onion, chopped
4 garlic cloves, chopped
2 medium tomatoes, chopped
1 teaspoon tamarind paste
2 teaspoons ground coriander
¾ teaspoon cayenne pepper
1½ cups fresh edamame
¾ cup coconut milk
1 cup water
Salt and pepper to taste

Directions:
1. Place the coconut oil in the Instant Pot and select SAUTÉ. Add all the seeds and cook for 1 minute.

2. Add the curry leaves, onion and garlic and cook for about 4 minutes.

3. Add the tomato, tamarind and spices and cook for 4–5 minutes.

4. Press the CANCEL button and stir in remaining ingredients.

5. Secure the lid and cook at high pressure for 7 minutes.

7. When the cooking is complete, carefully do a quick pressure release.

8. Serve hot.

Nutritional Information (Per Serving)
Calories: 586
Fat: 40g
Sat Fat: 24.6g
Carbohydrates: 37.9g
Fiber: 13g
Sugar: 8.4g
Protein: 29.4g

Rice & Lentils with Veggies

Yield: 2 servings
Preparation Time: 20 minutes
Cooking Time: 10 minutes
Ingredients:
1 tablespoon olive oil
½ teaspoon cumin seeds
½ of small onion, chopped
½ tablespoon fresh ginger paste
1 small potato, cut into small pieces
½ cup carrots, peeled and diced
½ cup fresh green peas, shelled
1 tomato, chopped finely
¼ teaspoon red chili powder
¼ teaspoon ground turmeric
Salt to taste
½ cup white rice, rinsed
½ cup split green lentils, rinsed
3 cups water
1 tablespoon fresh cilantro, chopped

Directions:
1. Place the oil in the Instant Pot and select SAUTÉ. Add the cumin seeds and cook for 30 seconds.

2. Add the onions and ginger and cook for about 2 minutes.

3. Add vegetables and spices and cook for 2 minutes.

4. Press CANCEL and stir in remaining ingredients, except cilantro.

5. Secure the lid and cook at high pressure for 5 minutes.

6. When the cooking is complete, do a natural pressure release for 10 minutes. Quick release the remaining pressure.

7. Serve with the garnishing of cilantro.

Nutritional Information (Per Serving)

Calories: 356
Fat: 17.9g
Sat Fat: 1.3g
Carbohydrates: 93g
Fiber: 20.8g
Sugar: 6.8g
Protein: 20.3g

Instant Pot Black Beans

Yield: 2 servings
Preparation Time: 10 minutes
Cooking Time: 30 minutes
Ingredients:
1 cup black beans, rinsed
3 cups water
1 tablespoon olive oil
1 garlic clove, minced
1 bay leaf
1 small onion, chopped
Salt to taste
Kombu - 1 small sheet

Directions:

1. Place the oil in the Instant Pot and select SAUTÉ. Add the garlic, onion and bay leaf and cook for 2 minutes or until the onion is softened.

2. Add water, baking soda, beans, and kombu.

3. Close the lid and cook at high pressure for 25 minutes.

4. When the cooking is complete, do a natural pressure release.

5. Discard kombu and bay leaf and add salt to taste. You can adjust the cooking time depending on whether you like your beans soft or a bit crunchy.

Nutritional Information (Per Serving)
Calories: 407
Fat: 8.4g
Sat Fat: 1.4g
Carbohydrates: 64.3g
Fiber: 15.5g
Sugar: 3.6g
Protein: 21.4g

Butternut Squash Risotto

Yield: 4 servings
Preparation Time: 10 minutes
Cooking Time: 7 minutes
Ingredients:
1 tablespoon vegetable oil
1 white onion, finely chopped
1 red bell pepper, chopped
1 cup chopped button mushrooms
3 garlic cloves, minced
3½ cups of vegetable broth
1½ cups risotto rice, rinsed
¼ cup white wine
Some ground pepper
2 cups butternut squash, peeled and diced
3 cups of assorted greens (spinach, kale, and chard)
1 tablespoon nutritional yeast

Directions:
1. Place the oil in the Instant Pot and select SAUTÉ.
2. Add garlic, onions, and bell pepper, and sauté until they turn slightly soft.
3. Throw in the risotto rice and stir well.
4. Pour the vegetable broth into the pot, followed by the wine, chopped mushrooms, salt, and pepper, and mix well.
5. Close the lid and cook at high pressure for 7 minutes.
6. When the cooking is complete, do a natural pressure release.
7. Transfer the risotto into bowls. Sprinkle nutritional yeast on top and stir. The mixture will thicken shortly, and be ready to serve.

Nutritional Information (Per Serving)
Calories: 412

Fat: 5.6 g
Sat Fat: 1.2 g
Carbohydrates: 75.5 g
Fiber: 6.6 g
Sugar: 5.9 g
Protein: 13.2 g
Sodium: 699 mg

CHAPTER FIVE

Poultry

Roasted Cornish Hen

Yield: 2 servings
Preparation Time: 20 minutes
Cooking Time: 19 minutes
Ingredients:
1 Cornish hen
Salt and pepper to taste
1 tablespoon olive oil
1 small onion, chopped
1 celery stalk, chopped
1 medium carrot, peeled and chopped
2 garlic cloves, chopped
1 teaspoon Worcestershire sauce
¾ cup water

Directions:
1. Wash the hen and then with paper towels, pat it dry.
2. Rub salt and pepper over hen liberally.
3. Place the oil in the Instant Pot and select SAUTÉ. Add the hen and cook for 2 minutes per side.
4. Press CANCEL and top with remaining ingredients.
5. Secure the lid and cook at high pressure for 15 minutes.
7. When the cooking is complete, use a natural pressure release.
8. Transfer the hen onto a platter to cool for 5 minutes before serving.
9. Serve alongside vegetables.

Nutritional Information (Per Serving)
Calories: 267
Fat: 12g
Sat Fat: 2.3g
Carbohydrates: 8g
Fiber: 1.7g
Sugar: 3.6g
Protein: 30.8g

Sweet Potato Chicken Curry

Yield: 2 servings
Preparation Time: 10 minutes
Cooking Time: 17 minutes
Ingredients:
1 tablespoon coconut oil
1 tablespoon curry powder
1 teaspoon ground turmeric
1 teaspoon cumin
½ teaspoon salt
½ teaspoon cayenne pepper
¼ medium yellow onion, diced
1 cup green beans
2 garlic cloves, minced
1 red pepper, diced
½ chicken breast, cubed
¼ cup chicken broth
1 sweet potato, cubed
1 tablespoon fresh cilantro, chopped

Directions:
1. Program your Instant Pot to SAUTÉ. Add garlic, onion, and oil and sauté until the onion changes color.

2. Press CANCEL. Add sweet potato, chicken, red pepper, curry, green beans, cumin, broth, turmeric, and salt.

3. Close the lid and cook at high pressure for 12 minutes.

4. When the cooking is complete, do a quick pressure release.

5. Serve with the garnishing of cilantro.

Nutritional Information (Per Serving)
Calories: 295
Fat: 10.7g
Sat Fat: 6.1g
Carbohydrates: 25.9g
Fiber: 6.4g
Sugar: 8.4g
Protein: 25.6g
Sodium: 758mg

Taco Chicken

Yield: 2 servings
Preparation Time: 20 minutes
Cooking Time: 13 minutes
Ingredients:
½ tablespoon olive oil
½ small onion, chopped
1 small garlic clove, minced
½ teaspoon red chili powder
½ pound skinless, boneless chicken thighs, cut into 1-inch chunks
8-ounce canned black beans, drained and rinsed
½ cup salsa
⅓ cup long-grain white rice
1 cup chicken broth
2 tablespoons cheddar cheese, grated
2 tablespoons fresh cilantro, chopped

Directions:
1. Place the oil in the Instant Pot and select SAUTÉ. Add the onion and cook for 2 minutes.

2. Add the garlic and chili powder and cook for 1 minute.

3. Press CANCEL and stir in chicken, beans, salsa, rice, and broth.

4. Secure the lid and cook at high pressure for 10 minutes.

5. When the cooking is complete, do a quick pressure release.

6. Remove the lid and transfer the chicken mixture into serving bowls.

7. Top with the cheese and cilantro and serve.

Nutritional Information (Per Serving)
Calories: 804
Fat: 12.7g

Sat Fat: 4.2g
Carbohydrates: 114.9g
Fiber: 19.5g
Sugar: 5.7g
Protein: 58.7g
Sodium: 872mg

Chicken Wings

Yield: 2 servings
Preparation Time: 15 minutes
Cooking Time: 15 minutes
Ingredients:
1½ pounds chicken wings
¼ cup tomato puree
1 tablespoon honey
1 tablespoon fresh lemon juice
Salt and pepper to taste

Directions:

1. Arrange a steamer trivet in the Instant Pot. Add 1 cup of water in Instant Pot.

2. Place chicken wings on top of trivet.

3. Secure the lid and cook at high pressure for 10 minutes.

4. When the cooking is complete, do a quick pressure release.

5. Preheat the oven broiler.

6. In a bowl, add remaining ingredients and beat until well combined.

7. Transfer the chicken wings into the bowl of sauce.

8. Coat the wings with sauce generously.

9. Arrange the chicken wings onto a parchment paper lined baking sheet and broil for about 5 minutes.

10. Serve hot with remaining sauce.

Nutritional Information (Per Serving)
Calories: 692
Fat: 25.3g
Sat Fat: 7g
Carbohydrates: 11.7g
Fiber: 0.7g
Sugar: 10.3g
Protein: 99g

Cajun Chicken Fried Rice

Yield: 2 servings
Preparation Time: 10 minutes
Cooking Time: 15 minutes
Ingredients:
½ pound chicken breast, cubed
½ tablespoon Cajun seasoning
½ tablespoon olive oil
½ onion, diced
1 garlic clove, minced
½ tablespoon tomato paste
¾ cups white rice, rinsed
1 red bell pepper, diced
1 cup vegetable broth

Directions:
1. Place the oil in the Instant Pot and select SAUTÉ. Add garlic and onion. Cook until browned, stirring frequently.

2. Press CANCEL, and add chicken breast, tomato paste, rice, Cajun seasoning, bell pepper, and vegetable broth. Stir well to combine.

3. Close the lid and cook at high pressure for 10 minutes.

4. When the cooking is complete, do a natural pressure release for 10 minutes. Quick release the remaining pressure.

5. Stir to combine before serving.

Nutritional Information (Per Serving)
Calories: 470
Fat: 7.7g
Sat Fat: 0.8g
Carbohydrates: 65g
Fiber: 2.6g
Sugar: 5.4g
Protein: 32.7g
Sodium: 487mg

Buttered Chicken

Yield: 2 servings
Preparation Time: 10 minutes
Cooking Time: 12 minutes
Ingredients:
2 boneless and skinless chicken thighs, cubed
½ cup heavy cream
1 tablespoon onion, minced
2 tablespoons butter
½ tablespoon garlic, minced
½ tablespoon ginger, minced
½ teaspoon chili powder
½ teaspoon cumin
¼ teaspoon salt
½ cup water

Directions:
1. Place the butter in the Instant Pot and select SAUTÉ . Add the chicken and onion. Cook until the chicken is slightly brown.

2. Add all other ingredients, mix, and close the lid. Cook at high pressure for 8 minutes.

3. When the cooking is complete, do a quick pressure release.

4. Serve warm.

Nutritional Information (Per Serving)
Calories: 479
Fat: 32g
Sat Fat: 16.3g
Carbohydrates: 3.6g
Fiber: 0.6g
Sugar: 0.4g
Protein: 45.2g
Sodium: 592mg

Cacciatore Chicken

Yield: 4 servings
Preparation Time: 5 minutes
Cooking Time: 15 minutes
Ingredients:
6 chicken thighs
1 large yellow onion, chopped
1 cup chicken broth
1 bay leaf
1 teaspoon garlic powder
1 teaspoon oregano
¾ cup black olives
¼ teaspoon salt
6 medium tomatoes, chopped

Directions:
1. Add all the ingredients to the Instant Pot, except olives.

2. Close the lid and cook at high pressure for 15 minutes.

3. When the cooking is complete, do a natural pressure release.

4. Garnish with olives and serve.

Nutritional Information (Per Serving)
Calories: 327
Fat: 18.5g
Sat Fat: 4.7g
Carbohydrates: 13.2g
Fiber: 4.1g
Sugar: 6.8g
Protein: 27.3g
Sodium: 641mg

Piña Colada Chicken

Yield: 4 servings
Preparation Time: 10 minutes
Cooking Time: 15 minutes
Ingredients:
2 pounds boneless chicken thighs, cut into small pieces
1 cup pineapple, diced
½ cup coconut cream
½ teaspoon salt
1 teaspoon ground cinnamon
¾ cup green onions, chopped
2 tablespoons desiccated coconut shavings
1 tablespoon arrowroot powder
1 tablespoon water

Directions:
1. Add all the ingredients to the Instant Pot, except for the green onions and arrowroot, and mix well.

2. Press the POULTRY button and cook at high pressure for 15 minutes.

3. When the cooking is complete, do a quick pressure release.

4. Add the arrowroot powder to a tablespoon of water, mix, and add it to the chicken. Let it simmer for a few minutes until it thickens.

5. Garnish with chopped green onions and serve.

Nutritional Information (Per Serving)
Calories: 572
Fat: 26.1g
Sat Fat: 12.5g
Carbohydrates: 14.9g
Fiber: 3.5g
Sugar: 8.0g
Protein: 66.9g

Sodium: 524mg

Barbecue Chicken

Yield: 4 servings
Preparation Time: 5 minutes
Cooking Time: 15 minutes
Ingredients:
2 chicken breasts, split in half
1 cup chicken stock
½ cup water
1 teaspoon nutmeg
1 teaspoon cinnamon
1 teaspoon ginger
¼ teaspoon salt
1 teaspoon pepper
½ cup barbecue sauce (use your favorite)

Directions:
1. Combine the salt, pepper, ginger, cinnamon, and nutmeg in a small bowl and rub the mixture into the chicken breasts.

2. Place chicken in the Instant Pot and cover with the water and the chicken stock.

3. Close the lid and cook at high pressure for 15 minutes.

4. When the cooking is complete, do a quick pressure release.

5. Remove the chicken and cover with barbecue sauce.

Nutritional Information (Per Serving)
Calories: 128
Fat: 1.9g
Sat Fat: 0.6g

Carbohydrates: 12.9g
Fiber: 0.8g
Sugar: 8.5g
Protein: 14.1g
Sodium: 719mg

Chicken Teriyaki

Yield: 4 servings
Preparation Time: 5 minutes
Cooking Time: 10 minutes
Ingredients:
1½ pounds boneless chicken breast
1 cup pineapple chunks
1 cup chicken stock
¼ cup brown sugar
1 tablespoon soy sauce
¼ cup apple cider vinegar
1 tablespoon ground ginger
1 tablespoon garlic powder
1 teaspoon black pepper
1 tablespoon cornstarch
1 tablespoon water

Directions:
1. In a bowl, combine the brown sugar, soy sauce, vinegar, ginger, garlic powder and pepper until the sugar dissolves.
2. Place the chicken breasts in the Instant Pot and top with pineapple and chicken stock.
3. Pour the sugar mixture on top of that. Stir carefully to coat the chicken.
4. Close the lid and cook at high pressure for 10 minutes.
5. When the cooking is complete, use a quick pressure release.

6. Remove the chicken from the pot, but keep the liquid.

7. Add the cornstarch and water to the liquid and stir until it thickens. Use as a teriyaki sauce over the chicken.

Nutritional Information (Per Serving)
Calories: 275
Fat: 4.5g
Sat Fat: 0.1g
Carbohydrates: 19.6g
Fiber: 1.2g
Sugar: 13.7g
Protein: 36.8g
Sodium: 507mg

Turkey Meatballs

Yield: 2 servings
Preparation Time: 20 minutes
Cooking Time: 15 minutes
Ingredients:
For Sauce:
¼ cup soy sauce
2 tablespoons rice vinegar
1 tablespoon canola oil
1 teaspoon fresh ginger, grated
1 garlic cloves, minced
1½ tablespoons brown sugar
½ tablespoon cornstarch
¼ teaspoon black pepper
½ cup water

For Meatballs:
½ pound ground turkey
2 saltine crackers, crushed
1½ tablespoons buttermilk
2 tablespoons scallions, sliced
½ teaspoon garlic powder
Salt and pepper to taste
½ tablespoons canola oil

Directions:
1. *For sauce*: in a large bowl, add all ingredients and mix until well combined. Keep aside.

2. *For meatballs*: in a large bowl, add all ingredients, except oil, and mix until well combined.

3. Make equal sized balls from mixture.

4. Place oil in the Instant Pot and select SAUTÉ. Add the meatballs and cook for 4–5 minutes or until browned from all sides.

5. Press CANCEL and add the sauce over meatballs.

6. Secure the lid and cook at high pressure for 10 minutes.

7. When the cooking is complete, use a natural pressure release.

8. Serve warm.

Nutritional Information (Per Serving)
Calories: 409
Fat: 24.4g
Sat Fat: 3.1g
Carbohydrates: 16g
Fiber: 0.7g
Sugar: 8.1g
Protein: 34.1g

Turkey Goulash

Yield: 4 servings
Preparation Time: 10 minutes
Cooking Time: 20 minutes
Ingredients:
2 pounds ground turkey breast
1 15-ounce can of diced tomatoes
2 cloves garlic, chopped
1 red onion, sliced
1 red bell pepper, chopped
1 green bell pepper, chopped
1 cup chicken stock
1 tablespoon butter

Directions:
1. Heat the butter in the Instant Pot and set it to SAUTÉ. Add the ground turkey, cooking it for 5 minutes.

2. Add the tomatoes with their juices, the garlic, onion, peppers, and chicken stock. Close the lid and cook at high pressure for 15 minutes.

3. When the cooking is complete, do a quick pressure release.

4. Serve warm.

Nutritional Information (Per Serving)
Calories: 508
Fat: 20.2g
Sat Fat: 6.6g
Carbohydrates: 11.9g
Fiber: 2.7g
Sugar: 7.2g
Protein: 67.3g
Sodium: 362mg

CHAPTER SIX

Meats

Meatballs in Gravy

Yield: 2 servings
Preparation Time: 20 minutes
Cooking Time: 43 minutes
Ingredients:
¾ pound ground beef
1 teaspoon adobo seasoning
Salt and pepper to taste
½ tablespoon olive oil
2 small tomatoes, chopped roughly
5 mini bell peppers, seeded and halved
1 small onion, chopped roughly
2 garlic cloves, peeled
1 teaspoon fresh ginger, minced
½ cup tomato sauce
½ cup water
¼ teaspoon red pepper flakes
2 tablespoons fresh parsley, chopped

Directions:
1. In a bowl, add beef, adobo seasoning, salt and black pepper and mix well.

2. Make golf ball sized balls from the mixture.

3. Place the oil in the Instant Pot and select SAUTÉ. Add the meatballs and cook for about 3–4 minutes or until browned.

4. Press CANCEL and transfer the meatballs into a bowl.

5. In the pot, place remaining ingredients, except parsley, and stir to combine.

6. Arrange meatballs on top of vegetable mixture.

7. Secure the lid, press the MEAT/STEW button, and use the default time of 35 minutes.

8. When the cooking is complete, use a natural pressure release.

9. Remove the lid and with a slotted spoon, transfer the meatballs onto a plate.

10. With an immersion blender, blend the vegetable mixture until smooth.

11. Select SAUTÉ and stir in the meatballs, salt, and pepper. Cook for about 2 minutes.

12. Serve hot with the garnishing of parsley.

Nutritional Information (Per Serving)
Calories: 496
Fat: 15.3g
Sat Fat: 4.6g
Carbohydrates: 34.6g
Fiber: 7.1g
Sugar: 21.6g
Protein: 57g

Sweet and Sticky Short Ribs

Yield: 2 servings
Preparation Time: 10 minutes
Cooking Time: 60 minutes
Ingredients:
½ tablespoon olive oil
1 teaspoon black pepper
2 short ribs, trimmed
¾ tablespoon garlic, chopped
1 tablespoon scallions, thinly sliced
½ cup water
½ tablespoon soy sauce
¼ cup barbecue sauce
¾ tablespoon vinegar
¾ tablespoon brown sugar
¾ tablespoon red chili paste
1 tablespoon cold water
½ tablespoon cornstarch

Directions:
1. Program your Instant Pot to SAUTÉ. Add oil to the pot and heat the oil until it is warm.

2. Add short ribs and cook for 5 minutes until they turn brown. Afterwards, place the short ribs on a plate.

3. Add garlic and scallions in the pot and cook for 1 minute, stirring constantly.

4. Add water, pepper, vinegar, barbecue sauce, sugar, soy sauce, and red chili paste, stirring the mixture to combine.

5. Close the lid and cook at high pressure for 45 minutes.

6. When the cooking is complete, do a quick pressure release. Carefully remove the ribs and place them aside.

7. Press SAUTÉ and simmer the sauce.

9. Whisk cold water and cornstarch in a small bowl. Add the mixture to the sauce and cook for about 1–2 minutes whisking constantly until it thickens.

10. Serve the cooked sauce over the short ribs and garnish with scallions.

Nutritional Information (Per Serving)
Calories: 1008
Fat: 86.6g
Sat Fat: 36.5g
Carbohydrates: 21g
Fiber: 0.7g
Sugar: 13.1g
Protein: 33g
Sodium: 756mg

Beef Burger

Yield: 2 servings
Preparation Time: 15 minutes
Cooking Time: 5 minutes
Ingredients:
1 pound lean ground beef
¼ teaspoon garlic powder
1 tablespoon Worcestershire sauce
Salt and pepper to taste
2-ounce cheddar cheese, shredded

Directions:
1. In a large bowl, add all ingredients except cheese and mix until well combined.
2. Make 4 equal sized balls from mixture and then with your hands, flatten each one.
3. Place about half of cheese in the center of 1 flatten ball and cover it with another flattened ball, pressing the edges together.
4. Repeat with the second burger.
5. In the bottom of Instant Pot, add a steamer tray and pour about 1 cup of water.
6. Arrange the burgers on top of steamer tray.
7. Secure the lid and cook at high pressure for 6 minutes.
8. When the cooking is complete, do a natural pressure release.
9. Serve with lettuce on hamburger buns.

Nutritional Information (Per Serving)
Calories: 544
Fat: 23.5g
Sat Fat: 11.3g
Carbohydrates: 2.1g
Fiber: 0g
Sugar: 1.7g

Protein: 75.9g
Sodium: 486mg

Beef Bourguignon

Yield: 2 servings
Preparation Time: 10 minutes
Cooking Time: 50 minutes
Ingredients:
½ pound beef stew meat
2 bacon slices
1 garlic clove, minced
1 medium onion, chopped
2 medium carrots, chopped
1 tablespoon parsley
1 tablespoon thyme
½ cup beef stock
½ cup red wine
1 large potato, cubed
½ tablespoon honey
½ tablespoon olive oil

Directions:
1. Place the oil in the Instant Pot and select SAUTÉ. Add beef and cook for 3–4 minutes or until browned. Set the beef aside.

2. Add bacon and onion, and sauté until onion is translucent.

3. Add beef and the rest of the ingredients and close the lid.

4. Cook at high pressure for 30 minutes.

5. When the cooking is complete, do a natural pressure release.

6. Serve warm.

Nutritional Information (Per Serving)
Calories: 559
Fat: 17g
Sat Fat: 5.3g
Carbohydrates: 47.5g
Fiber: 7.7g
Sugar: 12.3g
Protein: 43.3g
Sodium: 523mg

Instant Pot Picadillo

Yield: 2 servings
Preparation Time: 10 minutes
Cooking Time: 15 minutes
Ingredients:
¾ pound ground beef
½ large onion, chopped
1 tomato, chopped
1 garlic clove, minced
½ teaspoon salt
1 bay leaf
2 ounces tomato sauce
1 tablespoon olives, pitted
1 tablespoon cilantro, chopped
½ cup water

Directions:
1. Set the Instant Pot to SAUTÉ. Add beef and break the meat into small pieces using a wooden spoon. Cook until browned.

2. Add the rest ingredients and mix to combine.

3. Close the lid and cook at high pressure for 15 minutes.

4. When the cooking is complete, do a quick pressure release.

5. Serve with rice or side salad.

Nutritional Information (Per Serving)
Calories: 352
Fat: 11.2g
Sat Fat: 4.1g
Carbohydrates: 7.0g
Fiber: 1.8g
Sugar: 3.6g
Protein: 52.8g
Sodium: 883mg

Easy Lasagna

Yield: 2 servings
Preparation Time: 2 minutes
Cooking Time: 10 minutes
Ingredients:
6 ounces ruffles pasta
4 ounces ricotta cheese
4 ounces mozzarella cheese
¼ pound ground beef
¼ pound ground pork
1 cup pasta sauce
1 cup water

Directions:

1. Set the Instant Pot on SAUTÉ. Add beef and pork, and cook until browned and crumbling.

2. Add water, pasta, and sauce.

3. Close the lid and cook at high pressure for 5 minutes.

4. When the cooking is complete, use a quick pressure release.

5. Add ricotta cheese and half of the mozzarella. Stir to mix.

6. Serve hot and top with the rest mozzarella.

Nutritional Information (Per Serving)
Calories: 691
Fat: 24.1g
Sat Fat: 11.7g
Carbohydrates: 52.8g
Fiber: 4.7g
Sugar: 12.7g
Protein: 62g
Sodium: 997mg

Paleo Meatloaf

Yield: 4 servings
Preparation Time: 5 minutes
Cooking Time: 30 minutes
Ingredients:
2 pounds ground beef

1 cup salsa

1 teaspoon cumin

½ teaspoon salt

1 teaspoon paprika

1 teaspoon chili powder

1 teaspoon garlic powder

1 teaspoon ground pepper

1 onion, diced

1 tablespoon tapioca flour

1 tablespoon olive oil

Directions:
1. In a large bowl, combine ground beef with salsa, cumin, salt, pepper, garlic powder, paprika, chili powder, and tapioca flour and mix well.

2. Add the olive oil to the Instant Pot and select SAUTÉ. Add chopped onion and cook for about 1 minute.

3. Transfer the mixture from the bowl to the pot and give it a stir.

4. Close the lid, select MEAT/STEW, and cook for 30 minutes.

5. When the cooking is complete, do a natural pressure release.

6. Serve hot.

Nutritional Information (Per Serving)
Calories: 491
Fat: 18.1g

Sat Fat: 5.9g
Carbohydrates: 8.8g
Fiber: 2.3g
Sugar: 3.4g
Protein: 70.5g
Sodium: 839mg

Maple Smoked Brisket

Yield: 4 servings
Preparation Time: 5 minutes
Cooking Time: 60 minutes
Ingredients:
1½ pounds beef brisket
2 tablespoons brown sugar
1 teaspoon sea salt
1 teaspoon ground pepper
1 teaspoon mustard powder
1 tablespoon onion powder
½ teaspoon garlic powder
½ teaspoon paprika powder
1 tablespoon olive oil
2 cups chicken broth
1 tablespoon liquid smoke
Some fresh thyme leaves

Directions:
1. If the brisket is refrigerated, ensure you take it out and let it sit at room temperature for about 30 minutes.

2. In a bowl, combine brown sugar, sea salt, ground pepper, mustard powder, onion powder, garlic powder, and paprika powder.

3. Lay the brisket on a tray. Generously coat the meat with the above mixture.

4. Grease the bottom of the Instant Pot with olive oil. Heat for about 3 minutes on SAUTÉ.

5. Transfer the brisket to the pot and cook on both sides until golden brown. Make sure you don't burn the brisket while doing this.

6. Pour the chicken broth on top of the brisket, followed by liquid smoke.

7. Close the lid and cook at high pressure for 50 minutes.

8. When the cooking is complete, do a natural pressure release.

9. Serve with thyme leaves on top.

Nutritional Information (Per Serving)
Calories: 395
Fat: 15.1g
Sat Fat: 4.7g
Carbohydrates: 7.2g
Fiber: 0.4g
Sugar: 5.5g
Protein: 54.5g
Sodium: 613mg

Sesame Beef & Broccoli

Yield: 4 servings
Preparation Time: 5 minutes
Cooking Time: 25 minutes
Ingredients:
1 pound beef roast, cut in strips
2 tablespoons sesame oil
1 onion, chopped
3 cloves garlic, minced
1 cup beef broth
½ cup soy sauce
⅓ cup brown sugar
½ teaspoon red pepper flakes
1 pound broccoli
¼ cup peanuts
2 tablespoons sesame seeds
Salt and pepper to taste

Directions:
1. Set the Instant Pot to SAUTÉ. Coat the beef with sesame oil and season with salt and pepper, then place in the pot to brown.
2. Add onion and garlic and sauté for 2 minutes.
3. Add broth, brown sugar, soy sauce, and red pepper flakes. Cook another 2 minutes.
4. Close the lid and cook at high pressure for 20 minutes.
5. Steam the broccoli while the beef cooks in the microwave or stovetop.
6. When the beef is cooked, do a natural pressure release.
7. Toss with the broccoli, peanuts, and sesame seeds, and serve.

Nutritional Information (Per Serving)
Calories: 474

Fat: 21.4g
Sat Fat: 4.7g
Carbohydrates: 28.0g
Fiber: 5.2g
Sugar: 15.9g
Protein: 44.4g

Lamb Chops

Yield: 2 servings
Preparation Time: 15 minutes
Cooking Time: 21 minutes
Ingredients:
1 tablespoon butter
2 (4-ounce) lamb loin chops
1 small onion, sliced
1 garlic clove, crushed
1 (14-ounce) can sugar-free diced tomatoes
1 cup chicken broth
1 cup carrot, peeled and sliced
1 teaspoon dried rosemary
Salt and pepper to taste
2 tablespoons cornstarch
1 tablespoon cold water

Directions:
1. Place the butter in the Instant Pot and select SAUTÉ. Add the lamb chops and sear the chops for about 2–3 minutes per side or until browned.

2. Transfer the chops onto a plate.

3. In the pot, add the onion and garlic and cook for 2–3 minutes.

4. Press CANCEL and stir in cooked chops and remaining ingredients.

5. Secure the lid and cook at high pressure for 10 minutes.

6. When the cooking is complete, do a quick pressure release.

7. Meanwhile, in a small bowl, dissolve cornstarch in water.

8. Remove the lid and select SAUTÉ.

9. Add the cornstarch mixture, stirring continuously and cook for 1–2 minutes.

10. Press CANCEL and serve hot.

Nutritional Information (Per Serving)
Calories: 388
Fat: 15.3g
Sat Fat: 6.9g
Carbohydrates: 25.1g
Fiber: 4.9g
Sugar: 9.8g
Protein: 37.1g

Braised Lamb Shanks

Yield: 4 servings
Preparation Time: 10 minutes
Cooking Time: 35 minutes
Ingredients:
2 pounds lamb shanks
4 tablespoons white flour
2 tablespoons olive oil
2 garlic cloves, diced
1 large onion, chopped
3 carrots, diced
2 tablespoons tomato paste
1 tomato, diced
1 teaspoon oregano
1 cup red wine
½ cup beef stock
Salt and pepper to taste

Directions:
1. In a shallow bowl, mix the flour, salt, and pepper.
2. Dredge the lamb shanks through the flour.
3. Set the Instant Pot to SAUTÉ and add the olive oil.
4. Sauté the lamb until browned and transfer to a plate.
5. In the remaining hot oil, sauté the garlic and onion for 5 minutes.
6. Mix in the tomato paste, diced tomato, red wine, and beef stock. Stir well and bring the mixture to a boil.
7. Return the lamb shanks to the Instant Pot. Close the lid and cook at low pressure for 25 minutes.
8. When the cooking is complete, use a natural pressure release.
9. Transfer the lamb shanks to a platter and top with cooking liquid.

Calories: 609
Fat: 24.0g
Sat Fat: 7.0g
Carbohydrates: 18.4g
Fiber: 2.8g
Sugar: 5.8g
Protein: 66.5g

Parmesan & Honey Pork Roast

Yield: 2 servings
Preparation Time: 5 minutes
Cooking Time: 35 minutes
Ingredients:
1 pound pork roast
2 tablespoons parmesan cheese, grated
1 tablespoon soy sauce
2 tablespoons raw honey
1/2 tablespoon dry basil
½ tablespoon garlic, minced
½ tablespoon olive oil
Salt to taste
½ tablespoon cornstarch
½ cup water

Directions:
1. Add all the ingredients to the Instant Pot, stir to mix well.

2. Secure the lid, press the MEAT/STEW button, and use the default time of 35 minutes.

3. When the cooking is complete, use a natural pressure release.

4. Serve hot.

Nutritional Information (Per Serving)
Calories: 653
Fat: 29.4g
Sat Fat: 11.3g
Carbohydrates: 20.5g
Fiber: 0.2g
Sugar: 17.4g
Protein: 71.4g

Pork Wraps

Yield: 4 servings
Preparation Time: 10 minutes
Cooking Time: 25 minutes
Ingredients:
2 pounds pork shoulder, chopped
1 tablespoon roasted and ground cumin
1 teaspoon ground pepper
1 teaspoon oregano
1 teaspoon ground cinnamon
3 garlic cloves, minced
1 dried chipotle pepper
1 cup tomatoes, diced
3 cups orange juice
1 teaspoon salt
Some lettuce, sliced cucumber pieces, sliced onion
4 tortillas

Directions:
1. Trim the fat from pork shoulder and add it to the Instant Pot. Add the rest of ingredients except the lettuce, cucumber, onion, and tortillas, and mix well.

2. Cook this mixture for 20–22 minutes at high pressure.

3. When the cooking is complete, use a natural pressure release.

4. Transfer the mixture to a bowl.

5. Fill the tortillas with pork mixture, layering with lettuce leaves, cucumbers, and onion slices.

6. Serve on a large plate.

Nutritional Information (Per Serving)
Calories: 824
Fat: 50.1g
Sat Fat: 18.1g
Carbohydrates: 35.3g
Fiber: 3.4g
Sugar: 17.6g
Protein: 56.6g
Sodium: 754mg

Super Sausage and Peppers

Yield: 4 servings
Preparation Time: 5 minutes
Cooking Time: 20 minutes
Ingredients:
4 sweet Italian sausages
4 spicy Italian sausages
4 large bell peppers (any color)
1 15-ounce can diced tomatoes
1 15-ounce jar tomato sauce
1 cup water
1 red onion
4 cloves garlic, minced
2 tablespoons dried Italian seasoning

Directions:

1. Pour the tomatoes (with juices) and the tomato sauce into the Instant Pot.

2. Add the water, garlic, and Italian seasoning.

3. Chop the peppers and the onion into strips or chunks.

4. Add the sausages to the Instant Pot and top them with the peppers and onions.

5. Lock the lid into place and cook at high pressure for 20 minutes.

6. When the cooking is complete, use a quick pressure release.

Nutritional Information (Per Serving)
Calories: 370
Fat: 17.0 g
Sat Fat: 5.9 g
Carbohydrates: 26.7 g
Fiber: 5.1 g
Sugar: 15.1 g
Protein: 31.2 g
Sodium: 1028 mg

CHAPTER SEVEN

Fish and Seafood

Fish Curry

Yield: 2 servings
Preparation Time: 15 minutes
Cooking Time: 11 minutes
Ingredients:
1 tablespoon olive oil
1 medium onion, chopped
1 teaspoon fresh ginger, grated finely
2 garlic cloves, minced
1 tablespoons curry powder
1 teaspoon ground cumin
1 teaspoon ground coriander
½ teaspoon red chili powder
¼ teaspoon ground turmeric
1 cup unsweetened coconut milk
¾ pound fish fillets, cut into bite sized pieces
½ cup tomatoes, chopped
1 Serrano pepper, seeded and chopped
½ tablespoon fresh lemon juice

Directions:
1. Place the oil in the Instant Pot and select SAUTÉ. Add the onion, ginger and garlic and cook for 4–5 minutes.
2. Add the spices and cook for 1 minute.
3. Add the coconut milk and stir to combine well.
4. Press CANCEL and stir in the fish, tomatoes, and Serrano pepper.
5. Secure the lid and cook at low pressure for 5 minutes.

6. When cooking is complete, use a natural pressure release.

7. Remove the lid and stir in the lemon juice.

8. Serve hot.

Nutritional Information (Per Serving)
Calories: 787
Fat: 57.6g
Sat Fat: 31.4g
Carbohydrates: 47.2g
Fiber: 7g
Sugar: 8g
Protein: 29.7g
Sodium: 939mg

Shrimp Fried Rice

Yield: 2 servings
Preparation Time: 10 minutes
Cooking Time: 35 minutes
Ingredients:
1 tablespoon sesame oil
1 egg
½ medium red onion, chopped
1 garlic clove, minced
½ cup frozen shrimp, washed and tailed
½ cup peas
½ cup carrots
½ tablespoon soy sauce
½ cup brown rice
1 cup water
¼ teaspoon cayenne pepper
1 teaspoon apple cider vinegar
¼ teaspoon salt
½ teaspoon ginger, minced

Directions:
1. Set the Instant Pot on SAUTÉ and let it heat up for 2 minutes.

2. Add the sesame oil. Throw in the minced garlic and chopped onion and sauté until the onion turns slightly brown.

3. Slide in the chopped carrots and peas and cook for 4–5 minutes.

4. Add the shrimp, minced ginger, soy sauce, water, salt, pepper, and vinegar, and let simmer for 3–4 minutes.

5. Rinse the brown rice with water and add it to the pot.

6. Crack an egg into the mixture and stir well.

7. Close the lid and cook at high pressure for 22 minutes.

8. When cooking is complete, do a natural pressure release for 10 minutes. Quick release the remaining pressure.

9. Transfer the rice to a large plate and serve.

Nutritional Information (Per Serving)
Calories: 412
Fat: 12.1g
Sat Fat: 2.0g
Carbohydrates: 48.9g
Fiber: 4.9g
Sugar: 4.9g
Protein: 26.5g
Sodium: 702mg

Spicy Shrimp

Yield: 4 servings
Preparation Time: 10 minutes
Cooking Time: 5 minutes
Ingredients:
1 pound frozen shrimp, peeled and deveined
1 lemon, juiced
1 teaspoon black pepper
1 teaspoon white pepper
1 teaspoon cayenne pepper
1 can diced tomatoes (14–15 ounces)
1 jalapeno pepper, minced
2 cloves garlic, minced
1 sweet onion, minced

Directions:
1. Pour the tomatoes and juices into the Instant Pot.
2. Add the lemon juice, garlic and onion and stir.
3. Allow the frozen shrimp to rest at room temperature for 15 minutes. Then, add them to the Instant Pot.
4. Add the jalapeno and the black, white and cayenne peppers.
5. Mix everything. Close the lid and cook at high pressure for 5 minutes.
6. When cooking is complete, use a quick pressure release.

Nutritional Information (Per Serving)
Calories: 174
Fat: 2.3g
Sat Fat: 0.7g
Carbohydrates: 10.8g
Fiber: 2.6g
Sugar: 4.1g
Protein: 27.4g
Sodium: 283mg

Glazed Salmon

Yield: 2 servings
Preparation Time: 15 minutes
Cooking Time: 5 minutes
Ingredients:
2 (5-ounce) salmon fillets
Salt and pepper to taste
1 jalapeño pepper, seeded and finely chopped
2 garlic cloves, minced
1 tablespoon fresh parsley, chopped
2 tablespoons fresh lime juice
1 tablespoon olive oil
1 tablespoon honey
1 tablespoon hot water
½ teaspoon ground cumin
½ teaspoon paprika

Directions:

1. Season the salmon fillets with salt and black pepper evenly.

2. For sauce: in a bowl, add remaining ingredients and mix until well combined.

3. Arrange a steamer trivet in the Instant Pot. Add 1 cup of water in Instant Pot.

4. Place the salmon fillets on top of trivet.

5. Secure the lid, press the STEAM button, and cook for 5 minutes.

6. After cooking is complete, do a quick pressure release.

7. Remove the lid and transfer the salmon filets onto serving plates.

8. Drizzle with sauce and serve.

Nutritional Information (Per Serving)
Calories: 290

Fat: 16g
Sat Fat: 2.3g
Carbohydrates: 10.9g
Fiber: 0.6g
Sugar: 9g
Protein: 28.1g

Steamed Salmon

Yield: 4 servings
Preparation Time: 5 minutes
Cooking Time: 15 minutes
Ingredients:
4 salmon filets
2 cups water
4 Roma tomatoes
2 lemons
½ cup chopped shallots
4 sprigs fresh rosemary
Salt and pepper to taste

Directions:
1. Slice the tomatoes and the lemons.
2. Make two foil pouches with two pieces of salmon each. Lay the salmon down on the foil and cover with salt and pepper, olive oil, a layer of tomatoes, a layer of lemons, a sprinkle of shallots and a sprig of rosemary. Fold up the foil so it creates a secure little package.
3. Pour the water into the Instant Pot. Place the salmon into a steamer basket and lower it to the liquid.
4. Cook at low pressure for 10 minutes.
5. When cooking is complete, do a quick pressure release.
6. Carefully unfold the packets and serve.

Nutritional Information (Per Serving)
Calories: 495
Fat: 22.9g
Sat Fat: 4.6g
Carbohydrates: 13.9g
Fiber: 2.3g
Sugar: 4.0g
Protein: 55.9g

Mediterranean Calamari

Yield: 2 servings
Preparation Time: 10 minutes
Cooking Time: 4 minutes
Ingredients:
1 pound calamari, chopped
1 tablespoon olive oil
½ red onion, sliced
1 garlic clove, chopped
½ cup red wine
1 celery stalk, chopped
1 cup crushed tomatoes
1 sprig fresh rosemary
2 tablespoons Italian parsley, chopped
Salt and pepper to taste

Directions:
1. Toss the calamari pieces in olive oil and salt and pepper.

2. To the Instant Pot, add the wine, tomatoes, celery, rosemary, garlic, and red onion.

3. Place the calamari in a steamer basket and lower it to the liquid.

4. Close the lid and cook at high pressure for 4 minutes.

5. When cooking is complete, do a quick pressure release.

6. Remove the fish and sprinkle with fresh parsley.

Nutritional Information (Per Serving)
Calories: 332
Fat: 9.3g
Sat Fat: 1.0g
Carbohydrates: 12.5g
Fiber: 2.4g
Sugar: 4.8g
Protein: 35.7g

Steamed Mussels

Yield: 2 servings
Preparation Time: 10 minutes
Cooking Time: 3 minutes
Ingredients:
2 pounds fresh mussels, cleaned and rinsed
1 cup diced tomatoes
½ cup white wine
½ tablespoon pepper
½ tablespoon dried parsley
Salt to taste

Directions:
1. Pour the tomatoes into the Instant Pot with the juices and add the wine. Stir together and add the pepper, salt, and parsley.

2. Place the mussels in a steamer basket and lower it to the liquid.

3. Close the lid and cook at high pressure for 3 minutes.

4. When cooking is complete, do a quick pressure release.

5. Remove the lid and cover the mussels with the tomato and wine sauce.

6. Serve with garlic bread.

Nutritional Information (Per Serving)
Calories: 460
Fat: 10.4g
Sat Fat: 2.0g
Carbohydrates: 22.9g
Fiber: 1.5g
Sugar: 2.9g
Protein: 55.0g

Ginger-Lemon Haddock

Yield: 4 servings
Preparation Time: 5 minutes
Cooking Time: 8 minutes
Ingredients:
4 filets of haddock
2 lemons
1-inch fresh ginger, chopped
4 green onions
1 cup white wine
Salt and pepper to taste
2 tablespoons olive oil

Directions:
1. Massage the olive oil into the fish filets and sprinkle them with salt and pepper.
2. Juice your lemons and zest one of them.
3. Add that to the Instant Pot with the wine, onions, and ginger.
4. Place the fish in a steamer basket and lower it to the liquid.
5. Close the lid and cook at high pressure for 8 minutes.
6. When cooking is complete, do a quick pressure release.
7. Remove the fish and serve on rice or with a big salad.

Nutritional Information (Per Serving)
Calories: 274
Fat: 8.7g
Sat Fat: 1.0g
Carbohydrates: 5.7g
Fiber: 1.3g
Sugar: 1.6g
Protein: 32.2g

Cod with Parsley and Peas

Yield: 4 servings
Preparation Time: 5 minutes
Cooking Time: 5 minutes
Ingredients:
1 pound cod, cut into 4 filets
1 bag (10 ounces) frozen peas
1 cup fresh parsley
1 cup white wine
2 garlic cloves, smashed
1 teaspoon paprika
1 teaspoon oregano
1 sprig fresh rosemary
Salt and pepper to taste

Directions:
1. In a small bowl, stir the wine, herbs, salt, and spices together until blended.

2. Pour the liquid into the Instant Pot and add the frozen peas.

3. Place the fish into a steamer basket and lower it to the liquid.

4. Close the lid and cook at high pressure for 5 minutes.

5. When cooking is complete, do a quick pressure release.

6. The peas will be mushy and soft, so plate those first. Serve the fish on top.

Nutritional Information (Per Serving)
Calories: 234
Fat: 1.4g
Sat Fat: 0.3g
Carbohydrates: 13.7g
Fiber: 4.8g
Sugar: 4.0g
Protein: 30.3g

CHAPTER EIGHT

Snacks and Appetizers

Tangy Peanuts

Yield: 2 servings
Preparation Time: 20 minutes
Cooking Time: 40 minutes
Ingredients:
½ pound raw peanuts
1 teaspoon Old Bay seasoning
½ teaspoon kosher salt
2 tablespoons apple cider vinegar
½ tablespoon mustard seeds
1 bay leaf
Water

Directions:
1. Rinse the peanuts under cold running water and remove any twigs and roots.
2. In the bottom of Instant Pot, add all ingredients and enough water to cover the peanuts and stir.
3. Place a plate or trivet on top of peanuts.
4. Secure the lid and cook at high pressure for 40 minutes.
5. When the cooking is complete, use a natural pressure release.
6. Remove peanuts from the pot and keep aside to cool.
7. Drain well and serve.

Nutritional Information (Per Serving)
Calories: 659
Fat: 56.7g
Sat Fat: 7.8g

Carbohydrates: 19.4g
Fiber: 10.1g
Sugar: 4.8g
Protein: 30g
Sodium: 687mg

Applesauce

Yield: 2 servings
Preparation Time: 10 minutes
Cooking Time: 5 minutes
Ingredients:
1 large gala apple
1 large golden apple
½ tablespoon maple syrup
¼ teaspoon ground cinnamon
1 cup water

Directions:

1. Core and peel the apples before slicing them thin. Cut the slices into quarters, and place them in a large bowl.

2. Add the cinnamon and maple syrup to the bowl, stirring to combine.

3. Add water to the bottom of your Instant Pot before adding the apples.

4. Close the lid and cook at high pressure for 5 minutes.

5. When the cooking is complete, do a natural pressure release for 5 minutes. Quick release the remaining pressure.

6. Break up any chunks, and then serve or store in the fridge.

Nutritional Information (Per Serving)
Calories: 139
Fat: 0.3g
Sat. Fat: 0g
Carbohydrates: 33.6g
Fiber: 3.2g
Sugar: 28g
Protein: 0.1g
Sodium: 11mg

Marbled Eggs

Yield: 2 servings
Preparation Time: 15 minutes
Cooking Time: 25 minutes
Ingredients:
2 black tea teabags
½ teaspoon fresh lemon zest, grated
½ tablespoon whole cloves
1 cup water
½ tablespoon black peppercorns
2 tablespoons soy sauce
4 large hard-boiled eggs

Directions:
1. In a small pan, mix together all ingredients, except soy sauce and eggs, over medium heat and bring to a boil.

2. Remove from heat and transfer the mixture into a heatproof bowl.

3. Carefully, crack the outer shell of eggs slightly (don't peel the eggs).

4. Place soy sauce and eggs in the bowl with teabags mixture. With a piece of foil, cover the bowl.

5. Arrange a steamer basket in the Instant Pot. Add 1½ cups of water in the Instant Pot.

6. Fold a piece of foil in thirds to make a sling.

7. Use the foil sling to place the bowl in the Instant Pot.

8. Secure the lid and cook at low pressure for 20 minutes.

9. When the cooking is complete, do a quick pressure release.

10. Remove the lid and transfer the eggs into a bowl. Keep aside to cool.

Nutritional Information (Per Serving)
Calories: 161

Fat: 10.3g
Sat Fat: 3.2g
Carbohydrates: 4.1g
Fiber: 1.1g
Sugar: 1.1g
Protein: 13.9g
Sodium: 1050mg

Deviled Eggs

Yield: 2 servings
Preparation Time: 15 minutes
Cooking Time: 4 minutes
Ingredients:
2 large eggs
1 tablespoon mayonnaise
½ tablespoon olive oil
½ teaspoon Dijon mustard
¼ teaspoon apple cider vinegar
Dash of sriracha
Paprika to taste

Directions:
1. Arrange a steamer basket in the Instant Pot. Add 1 cup of water in the Instant Pot.

2. Place eggs into the steamer basket.

3. Secure the lid and cook at high pressure for 5 minutes.

4. When the cooking is complete, do a quick pressure release.

5. Transfer the eggs to a bowl of cold water to cool completely.

6. Peel the eggs and cut in half lengthwise.

7. Carefully remove yolks from egg halves and transfer into a small bowl.

8. Mash the egg yolks with a fork.

9. Add remaining ingredients, except paprika, and mix well.

10. Spoon the yolk mixture into egg white halves evenly.

11. Sprinkle with paprika and serve.

Nutritional Information (Per Serving)
Calories: 132
Fat: 11g
Sat Fat: 2.4g
Carbohydrates: 2.4g
Fiber: 0.1g
Sugar: 0.9g
Protein: 6.4g
Sodium: 139mg

Scotch Eggs

Yield: 2 servings
Preparation Time: 15 minutes
Cooking Time: 4 minutes
Ingredients:
2 large eggs
½ pound country style ground sausage
1 tablespoon olive oil

Directions:
1. Arrange a steamer basket in the Instant Pot. Add 1 cup of water in the Instant Pot.
2. Place eggs into the steamer basket.
3. Secure the lid and cook at high pressure for 6 minutes.
4. When the cooking is complete, do a quick pressure release.
5. Transfer the eggs to a bowl of cold water to cool. Peel the eggs.
6. Divide sausage into 2 equal sized portions. Flatten each portion into an oval-shaped patty.
7. Place 1 egg in the middle of each patty and wrap each egg with the flattened sausage.
8. Remove the steamer basket and water from the pot and with paper towels, pat the pot dry.
9. Place the oil in the Instant Pot and select SAUTÉ. Add the scotch eggs and cook for about 4–5 minutes or until golden brown from all sides.
10. Press CANCEL, and transfer scotch eggs onto a plate.
11. Arrange a steamer trivet in the bottom of Instant Pot. Add 1 cup of water in the Instant Pot.
12. Place the scotch eggs on top of trivet.
13. Secure the lid and cook at high pressure for 6 minutes.
14. When the cooking is complete, do a quick pressure release.

15. Serve warm.

Nutritional Information (Per Serving)
Calories: 516
Fat: 17.8g
Sat Fat: 12.9g
Carbohydrates: 0.4g
Fiber: 0g
Sugar: 0.4g
Protein: 28.3g
Sodium: 919mg

Prosciutto Wrapped Asparagus

Yield: 2 servings
Preparation Time: 15 minutes
Cooking Time: 3 minutes
Ingredients:
½ pound asparagus spears
5-ounce prosciutto, sliced

Directions:

1. Wrap the prosciutto slices around the asparagus spears.

2. Arrange a steamer basket in the Instant Pot. Add 2 cups of water in the Instant Pot.

3. Arrange any extra un-wrapped spears in the bottom of the steamer basket in a single layer.

4. Place prosciutto-wrapped asparagus on top in a single layer.

5. Secure the lid and cook at high pressure for 2–3 minutes.

6. When the cooking is complete, do a natural pressure release.

7. Serve warm.

Nutritional Information (Per Serving)
Calories: 125
Fat: 4.1g
Sat Fat: 1.3g
Carbohydrates: 5.5g
Fiber: 2.4g
Sugar: 2.1g
Protein: 17.3g
Sodium: 855mg

Carrot Sticks

Yield: 2 servings
Preparation Time: 15 minutes
Cooking Time: 3 minutes
Ingredients:
½ pound carrots
1 tablespoon butter
1 tablespoon honey
1 tablespoon Dijon mustard
1 teaspoon garlic, minced
½ teaspoon ground cumin
¼ teaspoon paprika
Salt and pepper to taste
Dash of hot sauce

Directions:
1. Cut the carrots into quarters lengthwise and then cut each quarter in half.

2. Arrange a steamer trivet in the Instant Pot. Add 1 cup of water in the Instant Pot.

3. Arrange the carrots on top of trivet.

4. Secure the lid and cook at high pressure for 2 minutes.

5. When the cooking is complete, do a quick pressure release.

6. Remove the lid and transfer carrots onto a plate.

7. Remove the steamer basket and all water from the pot and with paper towels, pat the pot dry.

8. Place the butter in the Instant Pot and select SAUTÉ. Add the remaining ingredients and stir to combine.

9. Press CANCEL and stir in the carrots.

10. Serve warm.

Nutritional Information (Per Serving)
Calories: 140

Fat: 6.2g
Sat Fat: 3.7g
Carbohydrates: 21.1g
Fiber: 3.3g
Sugar: 14.3g
Protein: 1.6g

Potato Fries

Yield: 2 servings
Preparation Time: 15 minutes
Cooking Time: 4 minutes
Ingredients:
¼ teaspoon baking soda
½ pound russet potatoes, peeled and cut into ½-inch thick fries
½ cup vegetable oil
Salt to taste

Directions:
1. Arrange the steamer basket in the bottom of Instant Pot. Add 1 cup of water, 1 teaspoon of salt and baking soda in the Instant Pot and stir to combine.

2. Place potato fries in the steamer basket, standing vertically.

3. Secure the lid and cook at high pressure for 2 minutes.

4. When the cooking is complete, do a quick pressure release.

5. Remove the lid and transfer potatoes onto a large plate.

6. With paper towels, pat dry fries.

7. In a deep skillet, heat oil over medium-high heat to 350 degrees F and fry fries for about 2 minutes or until golden brown.

8. Transfer the fries onto a paper towel lined plate to drain.

9. Sprinkle with salt and serve immediately.

Nutritional Information (Per Serving)
Calories: 560
Fat: 54.6g
Sat Fat: 10.7g
Carbohydrates: 17.8g
Fiber: 2.7g
Sugar: 1.3g
Protein: 1.9g

Tangy Sweet Potato Wedges

Yield: 4 servings
Preparation Time: 15 minutes
Cooking Time: 25 minutes
Ingredients:
3 large sweet potatoes
½ teaspoon salt
1 tablespoon dry mango powder
1 teaspoon paprika
2 tablespoons vegetable oil
1 cup water

Directions:
1. Wash the sweet potatoes thoroughly and peel them. Cut into medium-sized wedges.

2. Add 1 cup water and place a trivet in the Instant Pot.

3. Lay the sweet potato wedges on it and cook at high pressure for 15 minutes.

4. When done, use a quick pressure release.

5. Remove and place the wedges on a plate.

6. Heat the vegetable oil in a saucepan over medium-high heat. Slide in the sweet potato wedges and pan sear until they turn brown.

7. Combine dry mango powder, salt, and paprika in a bowl and mix well.

8. Coat the wedges generously with this mixture and serve.

Nutritional Information (Per Serving)
Calories: 162
Fat: 6.9g
Sat Fat: 1.3g
Carbohydrates: 25.9g
Fiber: 3.3g
Sugar: 6.0g
Protein: 1.6g

Sodium: 325mg

Creamy Artichoke Dip

Yield: 6 servings
Preparation Time: 15 minutes
Cooking Time: 3 minutes
Ingredients:
½ cup cannellini beans, soaked for about 4 hours
1 cup vegetable broth
8 medium sized artichokes
2 garlic cloves, minced
½ lemon
¾ cup plain yogurt
¾ teaspoon salt
¼ teaspoon ground pepper
½ cup grated ricotta cheese
Some nachos

Directions:
1. Wash the artichokes under running water and slice into halves.
2. Boil artichokes in water for 30 minutes. Remove the leaves and carefully remove the chokes using a spoon.
3. Add the artichokes to an Instant Pot. Add the minced garlic cloves, lemon, vegetable broth, and beans and mix well.
4. Secure the lid and cook at high pressure for 20 minutes.
5. When the cooking is complete, do a natural pressure release.
6. Open the lid and let the mixture stand for a few minutes. Now add yogurt, ground pepper, salt, and cheese and mix well.
7. Add these ingredients to a blender and combine until it forms a smooth paste.

8. Serve along with some nachos.

Nutritional Information (Per Serving)
Calories: 191
Fat: 2.6g
Sat Fat: 1.5g
Carbohydrates: 31.4g
Fiber: 13.2g
Sugar: 4.5g
Protein: 14.2g
Sodium: 630mg

CHAPTER NINE

Dessert

Stuffed Peaches

Yield: 2 servings
Preparation Time: 20 minutes
Cooking Time: 6 minutes
Ingredients:
¾ cup Amaretti cookies
1½ tablespoons almonds
1 tablespoon butter, melted
½ teaspoon fresh lemon zest, grated
2 ripe and firm peaches, halved and pitted
1 cup red wine
2 tablespoons sugar

Directions:
1. In a food chopper, add cookies and almonds and pulse until chopped. Transfer cookies mixture into a bowl.

2. Add butter and lemon zest, and pulse until well combined.

3. With a melon-baller, make the pit cavity of each peach a little bigger.

4. Fill the cavity of each peach with cookie mixture and dust with remaining cookie mixture.

5. In the bottom of Instant Pot, place the wine and sugar and stir to combine. Arrange a steamer basket on top of wine mixture.

6. Place the peaches into the steamer basket.

7. Secure the lid and cook at high pressure for 3 minutes.

8. When the cooking is complete, do a quick pressure release.

9. Remove the lid and carefully, transfer peaches onto a serving platter.

10. Remove the steamer basket from Instant Pot.

11. Select SAUTÉ and cook for 2–3 minutes or until wine sauce becomes thick.

12. Press CANCEL and pour wine sauce over peaches.

13. Serve warm.

Nutritional Information (Per Serving)
Calories: 549
Fat: 17g
Sat Fat: 3.8g
Carbohydrates: 74.6g
Fiber: 4.8g
Sugar: 65.6g
Protein: 6.3g
Sodium: 66mg

Braised Apples

Yield: 2 servings
Preparation Time: 15 minutes
Cooking Time: 10 minutes
Ingredients:
2 apples, cored
½ cup water
½ cup red wine
3 tablespoons demerara sugar
2 tablespoons raisins
½ teaspoon ground cinnamon

Directions:
1. In the bottom of Instant Pot, add the water and place apples. Pour wine on top and sprinkle with sugar, raisins, and cinnamon.

2. Secure the lid and cook at high pressure for 10 minutes.

3. When the cooking is complete, do a quick pressure release.

4. Transfer the apples onto serving plates and top with cooking liquid.

5. Serve immediately.

Nutritional Information (Per Serving)
Calories: 245
Fat: 0.5g
Sat Fat: 0g
Carbohydrates: 53.3g
Fiber: 6.1g
Sugar: 42.1g
Protein: 1g
Sodium: 10mg

Nutty Fudge Pieces

Yield: 2 dozen fudge pieces
Preparation Time: 5 minutes
Cooking Time: 10 minutes
Ingredients:
1 12-ounce package of semi-sweet chocolate chips
1 14-ounce can of condensed milk
½ cup walnuts
½ cup almonds
1 teaspoon vanilla
2 cups water

Directions:
1. Combine the milk and chocolate chips in a medium bowl (make sure it will fit in your Instant Pot).
2. Cover the bowl with aluminum foil.
3. Pour the water into the Instant Pot and set the rack so you can place the bowl on top of it in the pot.
4. Close the lid and cook at high pressure for 5 minutes.
5. When the cooking is complete, do a quick pressure release.
6. Remove the bowl and take the foil off the bowl.
7. Stir in the nuts and vanilla until everything is combined.
8. Drop in unformed balls onto wax paper and allow to cool.

Nutritional Information (Per Fudge)
Calories: 157
Fat: 8.2 g
Sat Fat: 4.0 g
Carbohydrates: 18.1 g
Fiber: 0.9 g
Sugar: 16.4 g
Protein: 3.4 g
Sodium: 32 mg

Lavender Crème Brule

Yield: 2 servings
Preparation Time: 5 minutes
Cooking Time: 10 minutes
Ingredients:

2 egg yolks

2/3 cup heavy cream

2 teaspoons sugar

2 teaspoons vanilla extract

Pinch of food grade lavender buds

2 teaspoons sugar, to garnish

Directions:

1. In a saucepan, add the heavy cream and sugar. Heat over medium heat to dissolve the sugar. Allow it to cool to room temperature.

2. Whisk your cream mixture with egg yolks.

3. Add the vanilla extract and lavender buds. Mix, then divide into two ramekins.

4. Arrange a trivet in the Instant Pot. Add 1 cup of water in the Instant Pot.

5. Place the ramekins on top of trivet.

6. Secure the lid and cook at high pressure for 10 minutes.

7. When the cooking is complete, use a natural pressure release.

8. Cool for at least 45 minutes before serving.

9. Garnish with sugar.

Nutritional Information (Per Serving)
Calories: 234
Fat: 19.3g
Sat Fat: 10.8g
Carbohydrates: 10.3g
Fiber: 0g
Sugar: 8.7g

Protein: 3.5g
Sodium: 24mg

Glazed Pears

Yield: 2 servings
Preparation Time: 15 minutes
Cooking Time: 10 minutes
Ingredients:
13-ounce grape juice
6-ounce currant jelly
1 tablespoon fresh lemon
½ teaspoon fresh lemon zest, grated
2 pears
¼ of a vanilla bean
2 peppercorns
1 rosemary sprig

Directions:
1. In the bottom of Instant Pot, mix together the grape juice, jelly, lemon juice and zest.
2. Dip each pear in juice mixture and coat evenly.
3. Wrap each pear in a piece of foil.
4. Add peppercorns, rosemary, and vanilla bean into the juice mixture.
5. Arrange a steamer basket over juice mixture.
6. Place the pears into steamer basket.
7. Secure the lid and cook at high pressure for 10 minutes.
8. When the cooking is complete, do a quick pressure release.
9. Transfer the pears onto a platter. Unwrap the pears and arrange in pudding bowls.
10. Top each pear with the spicy cooking liquid and serve.

Nutritional Information (Per Serving)
Calories: 241
Fat: 0.7g
Sat Fat: 0.1g
Carbohydrates: 60.4g
Fiber: 10.4g
Sugar: 43.2g
Protein: 3g
Sodium: 7mg

Squash Pies

Yield: 2 servings
Preparation Time: 20 minutes
Cooking Time: 14 minutes
Ingredients:
½ pound butternut squash, peeled and cubed
¼ cup whole milk
3 tablespoons maple syrup
1 egg
¼ teaspoon ground cinnamon
⅛ teaspoon ground ginger
Pinch of ground cloves
Pinch of salt
¼ tablespoon cornstarch
2 tablespoons whipped cream

Directions:

1. Arrange a steamer basket in the Instant Pot. Add 1 cup of water in the Instant Pot.

2. Place squash cubes in the steamer basket.

3. Secure the lid and cook at high pressure for 4 minutes.

4. When the cooking is complete, do a natural pressure release.

5. Remove the lid and through a strainer, drain the squash cubes and keep aside to cool.

6. Transfer squash in to a bowl and with a fork, mash slightly.

7. Add maple syrup, milk, egg, spices, and salt and mix well.

8. Place the mixture into 2 ramekins.

9. Arrange a steamer trivet in the Instant Pot. Add 1 cup of water in the Instant Pot.

10. Place the ramekins on top of trivet.

11. Secure the lid and cook at high pressure for 10 minutes.

12. When the cooking is complete, do a quick pressure release.

13. Transfer the ramekins onto a wire rack to cool.

14. Serve with the topping of whipped cream.

Nutritional Information (Per Serving)
Calories: 212
Fat: 6.9g
Sat Fat: 3.9g
Carbohydrates: 36.6g
Fiber: 2.5g
Sugar: 22.1g
Protein: 3.9g
Sodium: 118mg

Chocolate Lava Cakes

Yield: 2 servings
Preparation Time: 5 minutes
Cooking Time: 10 minutes
Ingredients:
½ tablespoon sugar
¼ cup butter
2 ounces semi-sweet chocolate, chopped
1 egg yolk
1 egg
½ cup confectioner's sugar
½ teaspoon instant coffee
½ teaspoon vanilla extract
3 tablespoons all-purpose flour
⅛ teaspoon salt

Directions:
1. Grease two ramekins and coat them with sugar.

2. In a bowl, melt the butter and chocolate. Add in the confectioners' sugar.

4. Whisk in the egg yolk, egg, vanilla, and coffee before stirring in salt and flour.

5. Divide into the ramekins.

6. Pour two cups of water into the Instant Pot. Add a trivet, then place the ramekins on trivet.

7. Close the lid and cook at high pressure for 9 minutes.

8. When the cooking is complete, do a quick pressure release.

9. Dust the cakes with powdered sugar before serving.

Nutritional Information (Per Serving)
Calories: 562
Fat: 35.8g
Sat. Fat: 21.6g
Carbohydrates: 59.7g
Fiber: 2.4g
Sugar: 17.8g
Protein: 6.9g
Sodium: 356mg

Caramel Flan

Yield: 2 servings
Preparation Time: 15 minutes
Cooking Time: 12 minutes
Ingredients:
For Caramel:
⅓ cup sugar
3 tablespoons water

For Flan:
2 eggs
1 egg yolk
3 tablespoons sugar
Pinch of salt
1 cup milk
¼ cup whipping cream
1 tablespoon hazelnut syrup
½ teaspoon vanilla extract

Directions:
1. *For caramel:* in a pan, add the sugar and water, heat over medium high heat and bring to a boil, stirring continuously. Cook until dark golden brown.

2. Carefully, place caramel into 2 (6-ounce) custard cups evenly. Keep aside to cool.

3. *For flan:* in a bowl, add the eggs, egg yolk, sugar, and salt and with a mixer, beat until well combined.

4. In a pan, add milk, heat over medium heat until just warm.

5. Add warm milk into egg mixture, beating continuously.

6. Add remaining ingredients and mix well.

7. Place custard into caramel lined custard cups evenly. With the back of spoon, remove all bubbles.

8. Arrange a steamer trivet in the Instant Pot. Add 1½ cups of water in the Instant Pot.

9. Place the custard cups on top of trivet.

10. Secure the lid and cook at high pressure for 6 minutes.

11. When the cooking is complete, do a natural pressure release.

12. Remove the lid and transfer the custard cups onto a wire rack to cool.

13. With plastic wraps, cover the cups and refrigerate to chill for at least 4 hours before serving.

Nutritional Information (Per Serving)
Calories: 322
Fat: 14.1g
Sat Fat: 6.3g
Carbohydrates: 40.9g
Fiber: 0.2g
Sugar: 39.4g
Protein: 0.2g
Sodium: 191mg

Vanilla Custard

Yield: 2 servings
Preparation Time: 15 minutes
Cooking Time: 6 minutes
Ingredients:
4 large egg yolks
3 tablespoons granulated sugar
½ teaspoon vanilla extract
Pinch of salt
1 cup cream
½ teaspoon ground cinnamon

Directions:

1. In a large bowl, add the egg yolks, granulated sugar, vanilla, and salt and beat until well combined.

2. Add the cream and beat until well combined.

3. With a strainer, strain the mixture, stirring continuously.

4. Transfer the mixture into 2 large ramekins.

5. Cover the ramekins with foil.

6. Arrange a steamer trivet in the Instant Pot. Add 1½ cups of water in the Instant Pot.

7. Place the ramekins on top of trivet.

8. Secure the lid and cook at high pressure for 6 minutes.

9. When the cooking is complete, do a quick pressure release.

10. Remove the lid and transfer the ramekins onto a wire rack to cool.

11. With plastic wrap, cover the ramekins and refrigerate for at least 3 hours.

12. Sprinkle with cinnamon before serving.

Nutritional Information (Per Serving)
Calories: 257
Fat: 15.7g
Sat Fat: 7.4g
Carbohydrates: 23.6g
Fiber: 0.3g
Sugar: 20.7g
Protein: 6.4g
Sodium: 133mg

Pumpkin Pudding

Yield: 2 servings
Preparation Time: 15 minutes
Cooking Time: 35 minutes
Ingredients:
¼ cup coconut milk
1 teaspoon gelatin
⅓ cup canned pumpkin puree, drained well
½ egg
¼ cup coconut sugar
½ teaspoon ground cinnamon
¼ teaspoon ground allspice
⅛ teaspoon ground ginger
⅛ teaspoon ground nutmeg
⅛ teaspoon ground cloves
Pinch of salt
½ cup water

Directions:
1. In a pan, add milk and sprinkle with gelatin.
2. Place pan over medium-low heat and cook until milk is just heated through, beating continuously.
3. Remove from heat and keep aside.
4. In a bowl, add the gelatin mixture, pumpkin, egg, coconut sugar, spices and salt and beat until smooth.
5. Transfer mixture into a greased soufflé dish.
6. Arrange the trivet in the bottom of Instant Pot. Add 1 cup of water in the Instant Pot.
7. Arrange the soufflé dish on top of trivet.
8. Secure the lid and cook at high pressure for 30 minutes.
9. When the cooking is complete, do a quick pressure release.
10. Transfer the soufflé dish onto a wire rack to cool completely.

11. Refrigerator for 4–6 hours before serving.

Nutritional Information (Per Serving)
Calories: 114
Fat: 8.5g
Sat Fat: 6.8g
Carbohydrates: 8.3g
Fiber: 2.3g
Sugar: 2.5g
Protein: 2.7g
Sodium: 143mg

Tapioca Pudding

Yield: 2 servings
Preparation Time: 15 minutes
Cooking Time: 8 minutes
Ingredients:
½ cup tapioca pearls, rinsed
⅓ cup white sugar
½ teaspoon lemon zest, grated finely
1¼ cups milk
½ cup water
¼ teaspoon vanilla extract
¼ cup fresh strawberries, hulled and sliced

Directions:
1. In a large heat proof bowl, add all ingredients, except strawberries, and stir to combine well.
2. Arrange a steamer basket in the pot of Instant Pot. Add 1 cup of water in the Instant Pot.
3. Place the bowl on top of trivet.
4. Secure the lid and cook at high pressure for 8 minutes.

5. When the cooking is complete, do a quick pressure release.

6. After releasing the pressure, let the mixture stand in locked Instant Pot for about 5 minutes.

7. Remove the lid and with a fork, stir the pudding well.

8. Serve warm with the topping of strawberries.

Nutritional Information (Per Serving)
Calories: 436
Fat: 6.9g
Sat Fat: 4.1g
Carbohydrates: 85.1g
Fiber: 0.7g
Sugar: 50.7g
Protein: 11.2g
Sodium: 161mg

Strawberry Cobbler

Yield: 2 servings
Preparation Time: 15 minutes
Cooking Time: 12 minutes
Ingredients:
1¼ cups all-purpose flour
½ cup granulated sugar
1½ teaspoons baking powder
¾ cup milk
⅓ cup butter, softened
1 teaspoon vanilla extract
¾ cup fresh strawberries, hulled and sliced

Directions:
1. In large bowl, add all ingredients, except strawberries, and with a whisk, mix until well combined.

2. Gently, fold in strawberry slices.

3. Place the mixture into a greased pan.

4. Arrange the trivet in the bottom of Instant Pot. Add 1 cup of water in the Instant Pot.

5. Arrange the pan on top of trivet.

6. Secure the lid and cook at high pressure for 12 minutes.

7. When the cooking is complete, do a natural pressure release for 5 minutes. Quick release the remaining pressure.

8. Remove the pan and keep aside to cool before serving.

Nutritional Information (Per Serving)
Calories: 816
Fat: 33.5g
Sat Fat: 20.7g
Carbohydrates: 120.3g
Fiber: 3.3g
Sugar: 57.3g
Protein: 11.8g
Sodium: 267mg

Apple Crisp

Yield: 2 servings
Preparation Time: 15 minutes
Cooking Time: 8 minutes
Ingredients:
⅓ cup old fashioned rolled oats

2 tablespoons butter, melted

2 tablespoons flour

2 tablespoons brown sugar

⅛ teaspoon salt

2½ medium apples, peeled, cored, and cut into chunks

1 teaspoon ground cinnamon

¼ teaspoon ground nutmeg

1 cup water

½ tablespoon honey

Directions:

1. In a bowl, add oats, butter, flour, brown sugar, and salt, and mix well.

2. In the bottom of Instant Pot, place apple chunks and sprinkle with cinnamon and nutmeg.

3. Top with water and honey.

4. With spoonful, drop oats mixture on top of the apples.

5. Secure the lid and cook at high pressure for 8 minutes.

6. When the cooking is complete, do a natural pressure release.

7. Serve warm.

Nutritional Information (Per Serving)
Calories: 393
Fat: 13.4g
Sat Fat: 7.5g
Carbohydrates: 69.4g
Fiber: 9.3g
Sugar: 42.5g
Protein: 4.1g
Sodium: 236mg

Molten Chocolate Mini Lava Cakes

Yield: 3 servings
Preparation Time: 5 minutes
Cooking Time: 6 minutes
Ingredients:
1 large egg
2 tablespoons olive oil
4 tablespoons all-purpose flour
4 tablespoons milk
4 tablespoons sugar
1 tablespoon cocoa powder
½ teaspoon baking powder
⅛ teaspoon salt
Optional but recommended: ½ teaspoon orange zest

Directions:

1. Grease 3 ramekins with butter.

2. Add 1 cup of water to the Instant Pot and insert a trivet.

3. Use a bowl to mix together all ingredients. Blend well.

4. Pour the batter into the ramekins, leaving a bit of space at the top.

5. Place the ramekins on the trivet.

6. Shut the lid and cook at high pressure for 6 minutes.

7. When the cooking is complete, do a quick pressure release.

Nutritional Information (Per Serving)
Calories: 217
Fat: 11.8g
Sat Fat: 2.3g
Carbohydrates: 26.5g
Fiber: 0.8g
Sugar: 17.1g
Protein: 4.2g
Sodium: 50mg

Hot Chocolate Fondue

Yield: 4 servings
Preparation Time: 5 minutes
Cooking Time: 3 minutes
Ingredients:
One 100 g bar of dark chocolate
½ cup heavy cream
1 tablespoon sugar
1 teaspoon amaretto liquor

Directions:
1. Add 1 cup water into the Instant Pot and set a trivet inside.

2. In a bowl, add the chocolate, cream, sugar, and liquor and mix well.

3. Transfer the mixture into 4 ramekins and set them on the trivet.

4. Close the lid and cook at high pressure for 3 minutes.

5. When the cooking is complete, do a quick pressure release.

6. Take out the ramekins. Using a spoon, stir the mixture in the ramekins for about a minute, so lumps aren't formed.

7. Serve with fresh fruit on the side.

Nutritional Information (Per Serving)
Calories: 197
Fat: 13.0g
Sat Fat: 8.7g
Carbohydrates: 18.3g
Fiber: 0.9g
Sugar: 15.9g
Protein: 2.2g
Sodium: 25mg

Wine Poached Figs on Yogurt Crème

Yield: 4 servings
Preparation Time: 5 minutes
Cooking Time: 7 minutes
Ingredients:
4 large sized figs
1 cup red wine
¼ cup honey
½ cup assorted nuts (chopped cashews, almonds, and pistachios)
4 cups plain yogurt

Directions:
1. Pour the yogurt into a mesh strainer and place it in the fridge to drain for about 6 hours. Do not wait for too long or the yogurt might get too crumbly.

2. Wash the figs and pat them dry. Place them in the Instant Pot. Add the wine and sugar and close the lid of the pot.

3. Cook at high pressure for 6 minutes.

4. When the cooking is complete, do a quick pressure release.

5. On serving plates, add the yogurt crème, and poached figs. Garnish with wine syrup and chopped nuts on top.

Nutritional Information (Per Serving)
Calories: 433
Fat: 11.1g
Sat Fat: 4.1g
Carbohydrates: 54.1g
Fiber: 2.4g
Sugar: 45.1g
Protein: 17.3g
Sodium: 180mg

Conclusion

I hope you and your partner enjoy the Instant Pot recipes in this book. Cooking in an Instant Pot should seem much easier now that you have all the information you'll need. Now there's no reason for you to order takeout. When in need, just use your Instant Pot.

Finally, I want to thank you for reading my book. If you enjoyed the book, please share your thoughts and post a review. It would be greatly appreciated!

Best wishes,
Savannah Gibbs